THE RIVER HOBBLER'S
APPRENTICE

The River Hobbler's Apprentice

Memories of Working the Severn and Wye

Alan Butt

First published 2010
Reprinted 2013

The History Press
The Mill, Brimscombe Port
Stroud, Gloucestershire, GL5 2QG
www.thehistorypress.co.uk

British Library Cataloguing in Publication Data.
A catalogue record for this book is available from the British
Library.

ISBN 978 0 7524 5138 1

Typesetting and origination by The History Press
Printed in Great Britain

CONTENTS

INTRODUCTION

The River Severn, two miles wide at Tirley during heavy flooding.

The beautiful Wye Valley at Llandogo.

I intended this book to look at a typical year in the life of a River Severn 'hobbler': men whose lives depended on the bounty that the river could provide throughout the seasons. From salmon fishing, eel trapping and elver catching, to odd jobbing of all kinds. A hard life carried on by real countrymen full of humour and, most of the time, rough cider. These are my own memories and old stories handed down throughout the years.

Without the benefit of such wizardry as the television set, and with radios in their infancy driven by the weekly-changed accumulator, humour was handmade. Practical jokes took centre stage in the lives of the older men and were hatched in the dark satanic recesses of the local pub, and I have tried to illustrate many of these old pranks that go under the heading of 'wind-ups' in our modern society. However, there was a serious and very arduous side to the existence of these countrymen. Weather played a huge part in the constant struggle to provide both food and cash crops of all kinds. This applied to most countrymen as Gloucestershire was almost totally dependent on agriculture for employment.

Being brought up in the late forties and early fifties my greatest influence was from countrymen born at the turn of the nineteenth century, mostly middle-aged who had somehow endured the horrors of the First World War (or the not-so-Great War as I prefer to call it), and who had endeavoured to carry on the old traditions and work practices that they had known before. It is with some regret that the changes in country life that I have experienced in the past sixty years have not all been for the best.

No one now seems to have time to 'stand and stare,' children do not know a blackbird from a crow or a narrow boat from a trawler, old men do not have their own seat in the local pub, and cider comes in bottles with gold labels and fizz. Where are the boss-eyed children I was at infant school with? The children with ringworm? And what ever happened to scarlet fever, leg irons and your mother sitting in the hearth so her legs turned to red squares? I have not seen cockroaches in peoples' Rayburns for years, and now it is women who contract sclerosis of the liver from binge drinking gin and shots of something blue with an unpronounceable name. Oh the joy of ice on the inside of cottage windows, school clothes in your bed to warm up, and the thought of hand-milking three cows before walking to school in the morning. Where is the flitch of bacon that used to hang in the scullery, and the backache from churning the butter after school? Bring back the good old days!

The River Severn taken from Haw Bridge.

This is a light-hearted look at old tales passed down to me by men with great country values. Also in this small book are some very interesting photographs with scenes of our two beautiful rivers, past and present.

MY THANKS TO

Lorna Page (for illustrations)
The late Vic Jones (front cover, one of the last rivermen)
The late Lionel Gaston (a real countryman)
The late Alfie Smith (willow cutter and riverman)
Roger Brown from Llandogo (some photographs)

CHAPTER ONE

SCRUMPY
AND MY JULIE

Formal education had ceased for me at the ripe old age of fourteen. It had long been decided that I was to be loosely apprenticed to my father as a 'river hobbler.' Although I had been assisting him for some time my mother had never allowed this work to interfere with my schooling. Forget about your cobbling, smithing and farm labouring, this was the big time – a self-employed river hobbler. This coveted position was granted by the Lord of the Manor who owned the stretches of the riverbanks on which we were allowed to operate. These rights had been in my family for generations, being passed from father to son.

This position meant that you worked the river through the different seasons of the year, and of course each season brought with it its own hazards, ranging from trench foot to lost fingers, pneumonia and tuberculosis, coupled with the occasional drowning! Father and I had spent the time since Christmas cutting logs for the local pubs and cleaning empty cider barrels by rolling them through the village, partially filled with water and a length of heavy chain. We had also rabbited hard locally, which meant that we had sometimes a two-mile walk to what father called good grounds.

Father had a ferret called Spike who was the meanest, most vicious animal that I have ever had the misfortune to come across. This ferret was so mean it would not have given you a boil, had it had a neck full. One day my father – who would not hear a bad word spoken about this psychopathic ferret – was lifting it from its travelling box by the back of its neck when it suddenly lurched forward and closed its fangs through father's left nostril. As the blood ran down his chin he made great efforts to convince me that the thing was only trying to be affectionate and that in any case we would all have been very hungry this winter without him.

Personally I was dreaming of hurling good old Spike into the Severn and hoping above hope that an old Jack pike would slowly gnaw off his private parts before he could reach the opposite bank. Some years later Spike took to eating rabbit kittens in the ground instead of chasing rabbits out. We waited for him to surface for more than an hour, and when he did appear in the nets the old man just picked up a spade and severed its head from its body with his only comment being 'I got another good 'un coming on.'

Life was rather harsh and there was not much time for a boy of now just fifteen to stop and wonder at how these beautifully fragile snowdrops at the side of the road had managed to survive a severe winter and still appear like miniature angels. We were bound for our yearly visit to Burt Illes' cider shed. We had a two-wheeled cart that father had bartered for with the estate manager of the big house. To facilitate the barter dad had supplied twenty fresh Severn salmon for a banquet to be held there. This would be attended by all the local nobs as well as some visitors from London. The cart was in a poor state of repair but dad was an accomplished carpenter and it was soon one of the best on the riverbank.

Burt and his wife Nell, always referred to as Mr & Mrs by me as indeed were all other grown-ups, had two skills in life that were in great demand by my father. One was the manufacture of cider, the other was the manufacture of a heavy type of gauze for the making and repairing of elver nets, which were vital to the existence of the rivermen in the coming months. 'Whoa you old bitch,' dad shouted at Jenny, our old Welsh cob mare that was slightly overweight and had an uncanny ability to fart loudly with every stride. I hitched her to the spear-shaped metal railings that stretched the whole length of the cottage frontage, placed a nosebag over her ears and followed dad into the small hallway.

We were carrying the barter with us which included two plump rabbits, two sides of dad's own smoked salmon, some bottles of mum's plum jam and left outside was a large bundle of withies (willow sticks used for making runner-bean tents.) I had been coming to this house for many years and it had always smelled the same; stale cider, boiled cabbage and wood smoke. Burt smiled broadly on our arrival, exposing teeth that strongly resembled a row of condemned houses I had once seen in the Slad Valley in Stroud. His hands were hard, cracked and almost black from being pickled in cider for many years.

After the normal pleasantries father and Burt went out through the back-kitchen, which smelled even more strongly of boiled cabbage, into the backyard where soon the unmistakable sound of barrels being rolled on loose gravel could be heard. With the absence of the normal shout 'boy' the two kilderkins of cider were loaded onto the cart, causing Jenny to lower her sleeping leg and temporarily put back her ears in disapproval.

The thirty-six gallons of venomous liquid, known locally as scrumpy, screech and cripplecock, had a specific gravity of anything between five per cent and twelve per cent, and was responsible for the destruction of hundreds of livers and millions of sperm in the Severn Valley. The 'killing-strength' of the cider was determined by the type of apple used, the time that they fell and the ambient temperature during the 'working period' within the cask. Cider-making is not a very precise art and it is made with little more than apple juice and some sugar.

The apples used were specifically grown for cider-making, the best variety of these being the Kingston Black, but most types of apple were used except the Bramley which made the cider too bitter. Cider fruit was collected as fallers and raked up with a wooden-tined hay rake. The result of this method was that it ensured a liberal helping of leaves, snails, bird and fox shit and a large number of fag ends, Woodbines mostly. The cider fruit was then put through an apple grinder or a cider stone and ground into slurry, and the particularly noxious substance that this produced was then shovelled into the mats.

These mats were roughly-constructed hessian envelopes which were placed on the bottom board of the cider press and filled with the apple slurry. This process was repeated until the press was filled to the top board. A large wooden screw, powered mostly by the rotation of a small horse, pressed the envelopes containing the apple mixture until the juice ran through the hessian envelopes over the bottom board and into a sunken barrel under the cider press. The juice, now only fit for consumption by children and vicars, was then bucketed into clean barrels, racked up and left with the top keystone open so that it could work.

After several days fermentation would begin, and cider 'snot' appeared, boiling from the open keystone hole. A saying commonly heard in the local pubs was 'my scrumpy's got good snot on 'er this year,' which meant that fermentation was taking place at a good rate and all the impurities, including the aforementioned rotting leaves, snails, bird and fox shit and Woodbines, were now leaving the apple juice. After several weeks of snot removal from the tops of the barrels, fermentation would cease and the barrels could be bunged up and left to mature. Another saying often heard in the local pubs was 'I've bunged up already,' which left visitors (always referred to as emmets) wondering if the whole village was suffering from some form of acute constipation.

A story mother often told was of the Plum Jerkum affair. Plum Jerkum was another form of strong alcohol. Manufactured by exactly the same process as cider but exclusively from plums, it was rare and only came about when there was a glut of the fruit.

Old Doctor Price and his nurse Sister Brown had delivered babies and administered to the sick in the village for as long as anyone could remember. Before the advent of a health service the barter system was also used by the local doctor to administer health care and supply medicaments. A visit to the 'quack' was rare and cost the patient much-needed provisions, the amount based mostly on the gravity of the illness and the ability of the patient to pay. This could range from a cockerel to a side of bacon for the

critical. The produce would be left on an old low table in the porch of the doctor's house, and it was said that the general state of health of the entire village could be determined by the amount of supplies on the old doc's table.

On the particular week in question the table at the doctor's house was overflowing with every form of consumable you could imagine; from a bunch of flowers for the lady of the house in return for a stitch in little

John Walker's lip, to a very large ham for the birth of the Jones's twins. But something was definitely up in the village! The old doc was having countless visitations from normally hale and hearty men, which was most rare. All the men seemed to be complaining of a similar illness, with symptoms of partial blindness and hallucinations coupled with nausea and severe bouts of diarrhoea.

Suspicions were aroused in the parlour of the doctor's house and my great-uncle Lemuel was ordered to bring a sample of the Plum Jerkum that the doctor knew the men of the village had been consuming in copious amounts. A sample of the liquor was despatched to Gloucester Royal Infirmary for analysis and was found to contain heavy concentrations of amygdalin, a drug poisonous if consumed in any quantities. The village cider press was found to have been used at the same pressure required for apple crushing, and had smashed the plum stones causing the release of the toxins into the juice.

Doctor Price ordered that the entire batch, some one hundred and fifty gallons, was to be destroyed without delay. This was to be carried out the following weekend by pouring the contents of the barrels into the river. When the dreaded day arrived the bungs were knocked out and the Jerkum ran down the bank, over the mud and into the river, causing grown men standing on the bank to break down in tears, and George Pickford to emigrate with his whole family to Australia!

While the weather-beaten men deliberated on all things rural, Mrs Illes worked a crude type of loom creating her much-coveted material used for the covering of the elver nets. She called to me 'why don't you go and see our Julie, 'ers in the yard just home from milking?' Julie was a milkmaid at Hobbs Farm and was at home between the two milking sessions. The cowman and Julie milked forty cows between them by hand, twice daily, and she always joked 'that is one hundred and sixty tits per session you know.'

Julie was a heavily built girl, not beautiful but attractive, with the clearest and softest complexion I had ever seen. She was wide in the backside and large in the breast, built I think more for comfort that speed. She was wearing a headscarf tied under her hair at the back and a thick cardigan over a printed dress. We talked of boy-girl affairs, dances and the new car that had recently been delivered to the big house making a grand total of three in the village. I was excited by Julie having known her for many years and felt quite easy in her company. I had kissed her before, and once on the Sunday school picnic I had tried my best to rub the floral print off the top half of her dress. She did not seem to mind and I was only stopped when the vicar's wife, suspecting a bout of groping, advanced towards us up the aisle of the charabanc.

I began to turn the conversation more suggestive and provocative while all the time trying to peer down the top of her dress, of which the first three buttons were undone exposing a row of melted and ironing-deformed smaller rubber buttons on her liberty bodice. With heart pounding I made my move! My left elbow was awkwardly pressed against the shed slightly above her head, as I leaned forward and kissed the side of her face. This was the prelude to a full-frontal attack followed by a full cavalry charge down the front of the dress, between it and the liberty bodice. I could feel my already work-hardened hands snagging the small frayed fibres of her underclothes. Julie hesitated for a few seconds before unceremoniously wrenching my hand from her clothing.

She rounded on me sharply saying 'If you want some of that make sure you're at the dance at the village hall next month.' She moved off swiftly into the kitchen and removed a heavy tweed long-coat that was hanging behind the door. Placing it over her shoulders she passed by me again and disappeared through the small gate at the bottom of the garden and into the meadow. I was not too disappointed with the outcome, as it had certainly left the village hall dance pregnant with possibility.

After adjusting the contents of my corduroy trousers I was struck with the brilliant idea that if I inhaled an enormous breath I may be able to pass through the brassica-impregnated kitchen without having to take another breath. I slowly approached the back-kitchen door, taking as I walked two shallow breaths and one enormous lungful as I passed within the portals. I shot through the kitchen and on into the parlour with oxygen to spare. My father and Burt Illes were still sat at the parlour table clutching old stone cider mugs; the only difference I could see was that my father was now having difficulty in keeping his large brown eyes facing forward and maintaining any sort of equilibrium.

His speech would lapse into involuntary bursts of a foreign language, the like of which I had only heard from a narrow-boatman who came from Norwich. With my return, and some prompting from Mrs Illes, it was decided that we should make tracks for home. Father was almost unable to walk, but with some assistance from Mr Illes I managed to push him onto the back of the cart. He rolled the bolt of Mrs Illes' material under his head and closed his eyes. 'Get on home boy, it's starting to spit,' said Mr Illes as he untied Jenny for me.

I clipped the reins on her back and we moved off slowly. Within five minutes the 'coming on to spit' had changed to 'coming on to piss it down,' but we were nearly always wet and so it bothered us little. I put Jenny's nosebag over my shoulders, but father lay totally exposed with the rain drops bouncing off his face as we made our way back to the riverbank. Mother was not best pleased with the sight of two drowned rats, one so drunk that he rolled off the cart and into the large water-filled depression in the backyard that we had been meaning to fill ever since dad fell in it the last time!

CHAPTER TWO

RABBITS AND HIS MAJESTY'S MAIL

Rabbits were, for us, one of the most important food sources in these very lean winter months. Most of the bounty from our river was in short supply, no salmon run, no shad or sea trout and the willow was in its winter shutdown. Some eels were still being caught in our eel wheels, which are a kind of trap placed in the small streams that run into the main river. The wheels were cleverly constructed out of willow to form the shape of a bottle with a small opening at one end to allow the eel to enter but not to leave. They were baited with an old piece of pig fat or a chicken's head or any other rotting meat we could find. Father would sometimes resort to using dead mice he had caught in the barn or eel skins from a previous catch. These eels would mostly be taken to the fishmonger in Gloucester for skinning and icing down and then transported by train to London for making into jellied eels.

Rabbits however were the best food supply at this time of year and a useful barter to be swapped for something else. Rabbiting with ferrets and nets was cheap to do and cost only time and a lot of patience. Spike and the other ferrets were cheap to feed on boiled rabbit they had caught, dry horse oats and the ends of small children's fingers that ventured too close to their cages. My Father and I would walk miles in a day, from 6.00am until it was almost dark in the evening. We would peg down nets on every rabbit hole we could see on the raised ground just in from the river's edge then lift the corner of one net and slip the ferret in, quickly pegging the net back down behind it.

Sod's Law would sometimes allow that one obscure hole hidden under a bush would be missed and most of the rabbits would make a bid for freedom out of this precise hole. This would always guarantee a clip round the ear for me for not having noticed the location of the hole, though it was hidden deep in a bramble bush. I did notice that other children in our village had a left ear that resembled a cauliflower, or that of a rugby front row forward. I think they must have missed rabbit holes as often as I did, but I do think it helped to keep the ringworm away as no self-respecting worm would be desirous of receiving regularly delivered hefty clouts whilst merrily burrowing through the side of a small child's face. This then of course saved a dozen eggs being bartered at the doctor's house for treatment with the telltale bright blue unction.

One of our favourite rabbiting spots was a large bank father called 'Glory Bank'. It was partially covered in small bushes (an ideal area for ear clipping) with grassy patches between. It was the biggest warren in our area and was not rabbited by anyone else as father had what he called the rights from the farmer for past services rendered. As Glory Bank was about three miles from home and lots of nets were required to cover the bank we would take the horse and cart. So many rabbits could be caught that we would not have been able to carry them all home by hand, and more importantly it was a long way from the nearest pub for the lunchtime cider intake.

It was a clear frosty morning and first light when we left the house. Mother had made a full breakfast and the fire had stayed in all night so the house was warm. I was reluctant to venture out but father was a hard taskmaster and work was work, with only cider drinking taking preference to it. The iron rims round the oak sides of the cart were covered in thick frost which sent searing pains into my bottom, and my other bits and pieces down that end disappeared up into my chest cavity in a split second. Jenny was about as enthusiastic as I was, and would have much sooner had a day in the stable than rabbiting at Glory Bank, but she could only show her disapproval in the normal way which was to fart with every step for the first hundred yards.

We passed Julie coming home for breakfast after her first shift in the milking parlour but I was too embarrassed to do much more than just acknowledge her as father was with me . 'Best cow girl in the whole of Gloucestershire that 'un is, got a way of getting the best out of stock she 'ave, you'd do well to get after 'er boy,' the old man said, not knowing I was busting my arse to build up some sort of relationship with her. We plodded on as fast as Jenny's reluctant legs were prepared to take us. By this time my legs were numb from foot to waist and I am sure dad's customary dewdrop was frozen to the bottom of his nose, but he was a hard man and not at all fazed by anything the weather could throw at him.

We pulled the cart into the gate at the bottom of the bank, and father was up and off before it had stopped. Jenny stamped her back foot in disgust at having to be there at all and I took five minutes to prize my arse off the metal rail and get my legs to function. We must have netted twenty-five or thirty holes at one side of the bank and this should have covered that part of the warren completely. The evil Spike was slipped in under one net and the almost-as-evil Wilf under another. Father lit his pipe, I sat on a hessian sack with my hand over my left ear (just in case) and we waited for the outcome.

Dad used a method which he called slack netting; this left the net firmly pegged down but with plenty of slack netting to enable three or four rabbits to be caught at the mouth of one hole, a bit like a funnel. At this time of year there are few or no kittens in the warren so the ferrets cannot stop to eat them and must chase the adults out. Rabbits make a blood-curdling screech when they are chased by ferrets which is sometimes a good indication of the amount you are about to catch, and that morning there was a loud one. Rabbits were flying out hitting the back of the nets up and down the bank, now the work would really start.

We used a fishing priest – a type of small wooden club used for dispatching salmon. A small blow to the base of the rabbit's neck was enough to kill it without spoiling the pelt, which we needed to be in good condition for the gypsy Zac. Father could pull rabbits from the nets and quickly put his foot back on the net to stop any escapees whilst dispatching the one in his hand at the same time. He was truly a master at this game. I struggled on, with my hands sometimes bleeding from the bites and scratches scared rabbits inflicted, but could only manage half of what father could do. It was a good catch, forty or more from one side of the bank. I think some had escaped from my end of the bank but – with my ear still intact – I shouted 'no bolters!' and he seemed pleased.

Now the messy part started. The only good thing about paunching rabbits was that it was warm on the hands. We put the rabbits in hessian sacks and walked back towards the cart. Jenny had moved a few yards in grazing and was now standing on three legs looking totally bored with the whole thing. Father was also an expert at paunching rabbits. His pocket knife was as sharp as a razor and in one movement he could cut the animal and shake its guts out without getting any on his hands, leaving the kidneys in place each side of its back bone. One more snip inside the windpipe and it would all cleanly fall away into whichever bag I was holding.

Some went to bait the eel traps, some to be boiled up for the ferrets and the majority in a tidy pile under the hedge for Reynard the fox. On estate farms the leaving of dead fouls and animal guts in the hedgerow was encouraged to help the foxes survive for next year's hunting, and in some cases the estate would compensate tenant farmers for losses caused by foxes sooner than have the farmer shoot them, for which the penalties could be severe.

One side of the bank worked out, rabbits gutted and in bags and the sun well over anybody's yardarm, the time had come for the pub. Father would sometimes make a feeble excuse that he needed to speak to old so-and-so about something, but most times he would say 'I'm as dry as a bricklayer's knackers' (something to do with the cement dust I think) and off we would go. The pub was about a mile from the rabbit ground, which meant the time spent was neither drinking nor working, so Jenny was clipped along at a fair rate. Her annoyance at this was demonstrated by her bottom resonating to what I think was her own version of the Last Post performed by some spotty adolescent from a dark satanic mill somewhere in Huddersfield.

The pub was well known to father as were all its patrons – a collection of farm workers, hostlers, woodsmen and some village shop workers. I put Jenny to the trough on the village green, emptied her nose bag of oats into a small pile on the grass and left her to it. Dad had already bolted for the pub before the horse had stopped and would be on his second pint of scrump on my arrival. The landlord was a local man that dad had known all his life, in fact dad knew every man in every pub that could be reached by a horse in one day!

Sid, the landlord, had been a mercenary soldier in the Spanish Civil War and had met and married a Spanish girl by the name of Cara or Casa or something continental sounding. The men all called her Juanita which always had me slightly confused until I first saw her, and then all was revealed. She had only one enormous tooth in the front of her mouth which protruded down and out like a marble tombstone, Ah! 'One-eater' I got it now. I did not think it was very funny and as a child with childish thoughts I wondered how hard it must have been for her to go apple scrumping.

Plenty of gossip and laughs, five pints of rough cider for father – one for me – and we were off back to the Glory Bank. The result at the other side of the bank was much the same and a goodly number of plump young rabbits were in our sacks for the journey home. As the sun set, the frost that had barely left the ground all day began to pinch once more and three streams of hot breath followed our cart, well, four if you counted the one from the nether regions of the horse.

Stew tonight, I knew it would be stew as it was Tuesday and for as long as Pontius had been a pilot it had always been stew in our house on a Tuesday. As I fed, watered and stabled Jenny I could smell the broth wafting through the wooden slats in the barn. Mother must have taken the lid off the cauldron she used for the stew and father was about to get his first ladle full of the piping hot ambrosia. That summer Jesse Owens had won four gold medals, but even with my speed impaired by an abundance of wet pig shit, ice and horse piddle, he would have been hard pressed to beat my sprint time across our yard to the back-kitchen door. I always said that the smell of my mother's stew could draw you further than dynamite could blow you!

As a River Hobbler's apprentice there are the proverbial chores and at breakfast, still in a half state of sleep induced torpor, I would go through the jobs in order of priority. First job was the horse. Muck out, fresh bedding in, feed and water and generally tart her up a bit. Despite her obvious flatulence problems and her sometimes careless attitude to gainful employment, I loved that old horse to bits and sometimes, when father had been particularly difficult, I would spend hours sitting on a milking stool just grumbling to her about him. Perhaps she knew what I was saying and that is why she had attitude sometimes.

Time for the pig next. Pig poo out, fresh bedding in, feed, water; scratch its back a bit just to watch its hind leg go up and down with joy. As the present pig was a Gloucester Old Spot, whilst I was scratching her I would think longingly about mum's home cured bacon. Alas, no time for sentiment in our hard existence. Next, feed and water the fouls. We had Bantams, Moran's, Light Sussex, Ducks of the Aylesbury White and Indian Runner types, an old stag turkey called Albert named after the old prince, geese with knobs on the tops of their beaks – one of which pecked the postman so hard one day it drew blood and Father laughed so much he dropped a full quart of cider in his shed.

I think the postman was a townie and instead of standing his ground and driving his boot into the psychopathic goose he turned tail and ran, festooned in goose shit, feathers, and His Majesty's mail. Mother saved the day with a sharp blow to the goose's skull causing it to veer violently off its intended course (which was the inside of the postman's trousers). Mother retrieved His Majesty's mail from the four corners of the front garden and returned it to a quivering wreck of a man half buried in our hedge. We were expecting a visit from the local postmaster but it never came.

Next on my list were Spike and his grisly gang of ferrets. Rabbit's guts, oats and some of yesterday's milk that was nearly on the turn were their rations. I hated the smell of ferrets in their cages, it was like stale vinegar and dead meat. Eel wheels were the next job. Just a short walk down the garden two small rhines emptied into the river and our traps were placed there and pegged to the bank by a length of rope. The traps were emptied of their catch of eels, re-baited and dropped back into the same spot. Armed with the fresh rabbit guts from yesterday's catch I set off for the traps. It was a cold slimy job and sometimes the larger eels would bury their sharp little teeth into your finger and twist their slimy bodies up your arm. I knew I should have trained as a cooper or a thatcher!

In all the traps there were only a total of eight eels, three of which were bootlaces, and I chucked them back making five good keepers, one of which was a four pounder. With the eels safely in the sack, the next job was the skinning. We had a large oak door on our shed and I would hold the eel against the shed door and drive a large nail through the back of its head. With my very sharp pocket knife I would cut around the eel's neck just to the depth of its skin and, with the prong of an old dinner fork stuck through the skin, I would roll it back until it all came off at the bottom of its tail leaving a skinless eel hanging on the door.

Now the eel was cut off clean leaving the head on the door. Simple you would think, but no. Father was such a precise man that all the heads had to be perfectly straight, and when I was a much younger boy failure to ensure perfectly lateral lines usually resulted in some more thickening of the tissue of my left ear. On the completion of these chores the day's work could start.

CHAPTER THREE

GYPSY ZAC AND JACK

Dad had skinned all the rabbits from Glory Bank and added them to the other pelts we had collected from the warrens we worked throughout the season. The skinning was work carried out only by father; it was pure magic to see his huge hands used with such dexterity. He could – with two small cuts of his knife and the perfect pressure of his hands – pull the pelt completely off a rabbit without a single hole or tear in it. With a home-made sort of scraper thing he would then remove any fat, skin and slime from the inside of the pelt, rub in some sort of salt or saltpetre into the flesh side and place it on the pile he had made in the shed. This would then be topped with a flat board and a weight from an old scale.

Dad was so precise about this work that he would let no one else touch it, and till this day I am still not totally clear how he did it, or just what preserving mixture he used. I was not deemed responsible enough to be availed of these secrets at my age, and when the man who came to purchase the rabbits died father stop practising this art.

Two or three times a year a full-blooded Romany gypsy known only by the name of Zac visited our house. He would always come with two women – whom father said were his wives – and one or two very small infants or babies. The infants they came with were quite obviously not from the wives as they were many years past childbearing. Father always said that Zac was the head of the family or tribe. The main tribe would continue on to the strawberry fields at Cheddar and Zac would catch up some days later.

Zac was a most colourful man with skin the same shade as a leather belt dad had been given by my Uncle Tom after a seafaring trip to the Middle East. He wore thick corduroy trousers, a cream-coloured blouse and a waistcoat with the most exquisite embroidery all over it. Round his neck was a bright purple neckerchief, with another one round his head under a black felt trilby hat decorated with pheasant feathers. His hair and part of his headscarf hung down his back from under the hat.

The old women were also dressed in very colourful clothes but with black headscarves and small gold coins hanging in front of their eyes. All of their handsome faces were so weather-beaten and lined it looked almost as though they had been pickled. It was very difficult to determine their age but father could remember Zac doing business with my grandfather when he was only a small child. He said they looked about the same but that must have been forty years before.

They would pull their beautifully decorated caravan onto our paddock and Zac would see to his ponies and untack the cob that was pulling the caravan. A ring of stones was placed in front of the caravan and a fire would be lit, then wood frames for cooking pots would be placed over and beside the fire. Stools and a beautifully constructed bench were then drawn close to the fire and this was all set up within a few minutes.

The women never spoke to us, not even to my mother, but one day when I was about six or seven one of the old women slipped a square of something in to my hand whilst passing. She did it so fast without stopping and I kept on walking as I was quite scared of these strange people. When I reached the safety of the house mother and I examined the strange gift. It was a sweet, about one inch by one inch, and looked like the coconut ice I was to taste in later years. Mum broke off a tiny piece and tasted it. I could see her face light up and when she gave me a piece I could tell why.

It was the most wonderful sweet I have ever tasted, not that I had tasted many, but I have still not had anything like it since. Honey, perfume and sweet wood smoke seemed to be the main constituents, but we were not sure and we could not ask. Regardless it was heavenly. Mother made me walk in the paddock to see if I could thank the lady, because that is how we were brought up. I saw the lady go to the hedge to put out some washing, so reluctantly I approached her and on passing said 'thank you very much for the sweet lady.' I think I saw a tiny smile on her face but she did not speak or attempt to stop.

Zac had come every year since time began for the rabbit skins and other supplies that he may need, though mostly for the skins. The old gypsy would snare many rabbits for himself in his travels, but not on the scale that we did as he lived mostly on the move. After the family had settled in father would take a raw onion, a hunk of bread and a three-quart stone jar of cider and set off towards Zac's encampment. Dad would stop near the camp and wait for Zac to wave him in. It was our land but this seemed to be some old tradition that had gone on forever.

The two would shake hands and sit down by the fire while one of the women would bring out some old mugs and dad would start to pour cider for himself and the old man. There was a lot of drinking and then some spitting on hands and handshaking well into the late evening. The women never went near the proceedings and got no closer than the steps of the caravan, where they would sit smoking clay pipes of which the stems had been reduced by breakage until they were not much longer than the thickness of their lips. The clandestine meeting would end without much ceremony and father would walk back to the house much worse the wear for drink, but pleased with the deal he had made with Zac.

By dawn the gypsy campfire would be alight once more and there would be a lot of activity in the camp. Soon after this the old man would walk towards the house and father would beckon for him to come on, just as he had done to father the night before. They would disappear into the shed and emerge shortly after with a large heap of rabbit pelts, a pint of cider and a side of smoked salmon, but it could often be some vegetables or anything that we had a surfeit of and that Zac needed. The gypsy would smell the pelts as he walked and continually rub the fur; I think this to see if they were fresh and well-preserved, or maybe it was some old gypsy magic spell he was putting on us.

In a small cart towed behind the caravan and covered with a canvas sheet was a wood lathe. It was turned by some sort of treadle method by moving your feet up and down as if to ride a bicycle. Ancient metal chisels were then employed to fashion the most intricate patterns on things like spindles for staircases and spokes for small wheeled-carts and all sorts of decorative artefacts. Dad had some wonderful things the old gypsy had made, and the pegs mum had were very special and lasted years.

He also crafted small boxes out of wood and lined them inside with mother-of-pearl from the inside of the shells of freshwater mussels found in certain rivers and lakes. Father and the old man had a good rapport, and though not a lot of words were spoken between them I could see as I grew up that these men had the greatest of respect for one another. Dad said that our rabbit skins were treated in some secret Romany way and used for bed covers and clothing for swaddling babies in, and once I did see one of the babies wrapped in what looked like rabbit skin.

The trading successfully completed Zac and his family would be gone one morning, back to join the main tribe on their way to the strawberry fields of Cheddar, or back up for the hop picking in Herefordshire or some other part of Britain that needed seasonal labour.

When I was about twelve years old, on a wet spring day after my work around the house was completed I was looking for a new nut stick to make a bow. I walked through a small cider apple orchard next to our paddock and I could hear the sound of a young jackdaw squawking fit to burst. The noise was coming from a large fallen limb of an old pear tree, chock dog pears they were called, and the fruit used for perry making. On closer inspection there was a large knothole in the rotten fallen limb and the bird was inside.

What a sorry sight; half-feathered, cold, wet and just about to expire. This instantly conjured up memories of my grandmother and the day she caught her heel in the slats on our river staging and pitched headfirst into the river with only her old black lace-up boots protruding above the waterline. Mother and my auntie managed to pull her out, but with the weight of about forty layers of clothes she must have weighed about a ton. My auntie was taking her to Tewkesbury in our punt. Dad had said that he would do it but she insisted on going with auntie Bet. Father had heard the splash and was concerned, but on the sight of gran's boots sticking out clear of the water he had crumpled to his knees in uncontrollable laughter and was trying to roll behind the rhubarb so mother wouldn't see him. Years later dad would be mending our shoes in the kitchen and would giggle out loud then look round sheepishly, but mother knew what he was laughing about.

I put the jackdaw chick in my jumper and headed back to the house. I collected a wooden crate from the shed, lined it with straw and put the bird in the hearth close to the fire. 'It'll be dead by morning,' my ever-optimistic father said, but it was not, and as the next day was Sunday and apart from animal chores there was no work to do, I could devote some time to my new friend. In the morning the bird looked much stronger and when I placed my hand over him he would open his beak and squawk for food. I soaked some bread in milk and dropped it into his begging beak and he ate it greedily. This little bird is going to make it, I thought.

While feeding him I noticed he had what looked like a large sheep tick buried in the back of his head under the feathers. I told Father and he said not to pull it out as I may leave the head of the tick in the bird which could give it blood poisoning. Later that day father put a small spill in the fire, got it well alight, then blew it out and touched the red-hot smouldering end on the tick's fat blood-filled arse and it fell clean out on to the floor.

Jack I named him. Original, I know, but it suited him anyway. With chopped garden worms, bugs and bread and milk the bird prospered and soon fledged but did not fly away. He stayed around the house and gardens and was truly a household pet. My mother became very attached to Jack and after we had had him for about four years he could mimic mum's voice perfectly and followed her everywhere. He would bring her brightly coloured objects and put them on the bed if the upstairs windows were left open. All the antics of the bird were carefully scrutinized by Zac, the gypsy, every time he visited the house but I thought nothing of it.

Jack was a real character and would follow me to every job we went on, even out into the river fishing, and before I had left school he was banned from the classroom and I had a hell of a job to keep him away. One day Jack put a gold ring in an imaginary nest he had built on some old rags in the scullery and squawked extra loudly at mother to go and see his triumph. Mum saw the ring and was thrown instantly into a panic. 'He's gone and done it now,' she said, 'he's gone and stolen someone's wedding ring and the police will be here in a moment!'

The Seatons ran the village bakers and Old Mother Seaton was at least twenty stone with an arse like a bay window. She was no stranger to the odd pie or pasty, you could see that. She would hustle and bustle along the village in a huge white starched apron, that when she was not using doubled up as the topsail on HMS *Victory*. Mother Seaton made the cakes and pastries while her long suffering and very skinny husband, Sacky Seaton, made the bread. Old Mother Seaton always took off her wedding ring before kneading pastry dough and placed it on the window sill. This was because it was said that she had almost choked the vicar once after her ring had found its way into one of his Chelseas.

It was a hot summer's day and Old Mother Seaton, being prone to the odd bouts of sweating, due to her weight more than her time of life, had opened the windows. Jack had not missed the opportunity to fly in and steal the ring. After extensive investigations in the village the affair was resolved without prosecution of the bird and with a large bag of cakes for us!

Jack was now an accomplished bird at mimicking voices and sounds and stealing anything bright or colourful. He must have been about eight years old and I was just about to leave home. Then, as he had done for forty or fifty years, Zac, the gypsy, turned up one day and the same old ritual of cider drinking and bartering began in the paddock, and although I was in my early twenties I was still excluded. Somehow the negotiations seemed longer and more passionate than ever before but I didn't know why.

Deals done Zac left early next morning and at breakfast I asked father if the barter had seemed difficult this time. Now I was twenty and able to do a good day's work he would talk to me about things. 'Very,' he said. The old gypsy wanted to buy Jack and was prepared to swap dad a gold Hunter watch for him. That is why for years the old man had taken such an interest in Jack and his antics. I think if I had been younger and my mother had not have been so attached he just may have let him go but thank God he did not. Some years after that Zac stopped coming to the house, and before long the Romany gypsies stopped coming through the village all together.

Before they did however, as a young newly married man I walked up to a man at the head of the gypsy convoy, told him who I was, and asked what had happened to Zac. The man, dressed similarly to how Zac used to, was walking along beside the shafts of his caravan and did not slow down or look at me very much. He replied, 'I know who you are. I used to come to your house when I was a young 'un. Zac died three years ago and there was a big wake held at Evesham, everybody came. Good man your father is, Zac said so.' He walked on, never looking back, and soon these honourable people were gone forever.

CHAPTER FOUR

WILLOW, MUD
AND UNCLE TOM

The willow was our chief source of cash-money and vital for us to obtain the things for which we were unable to barter. There is nothing romantic about the willow. In fact it is a rather ugly wetland dweller, raved about only by tawny owls that use its gnarled and hollow trunks for nest-building and spying on twilight walkers and unsuspecting voles.

The names of things on the riverbank varied from place to place, and often more than one name was used for the same item in a different state of maturity. The willow, withy and perches were all names used for this wet-footed easy-growing tree. My grandfather had laid down some of the perch beds that father and I were still working. To form these beds from which the withies were cut, branches from mature willow trees were cut into four-foot lengths the thickness of a fence post. These cords as they were called were then sharpened at one end and driven into the mud just above high-water line and below flood level. This was an inhospitable strip of land that was kept wet by high tides, by which we were still influenced, although many miles upriver, and the inevitable continuous winter flooding.

After a few weeks the stakes began to sprout from their entire length, showing the ease of propagation of this tree. The shoots at the sides of the stakes were trimmed off and only the growth on the top rim was left. In March and April the small thin shoots were cut for the weaving of baskets. Some were left for two years to grow larger and were used as stretchers to make the frame of the basket. Salmon putchers were also constructed in the same way and almost a third of our crop went to the salmon fishermen further down the river.

Cutting was labour-intensive and dangerous. The shoots were gathered into a bundle with one arm and hacked off with a very sharp hacker (billhook) with the other hand. The danger was that if you overestimated the power needed to cut the bundle, the hacker would continue on through and bury itself in your chest, or if the blow was too high the result was a severed little finger. The bundles were tied with lengths of willow bark and transported either on our cart to the basket-makers or by narrow boat to the fishermen downriver. Very much further south than us in the Somerset Levels willow-growing was on a vast scale, carried out by heeling in thousands of willow twigs into a bog and cutting them by the ton with tools like a hook and crook when they reached the required size.

Cut willow arriving at Newnham-on-Severn for the building of putchers and kypes.

In early April father and I were working in the perch beds cutting small weaving sticks to fill a contract given to us by the basket-makers. The mud on the bank had been unbearable for the past month due to a very wet time in February. It filled my boots, caked my trousers and made me wish I were a thatcher up in the Cotswolds. Father however seemed to love mud and was totally at home in it. He wore putties, strips of canvas wound around his legs from the top of his boots to just below his knees; the mud created a seal over the canvas and stopped most of the wet penetrating his legs and boots. My father never talked about the Great War at home, as though the horrific conditions were too ghastly to be expressed in any meaningful terms, but I once heard him say to one of the men in a pub that nearly as many men were killed by the mud as were killed by German fire.

I had just stopped cutting to sharpen my hacker when I heard a sound that had always filled me with excitement and anticipation. It was the unmistakable puffing of Uncle Tom's steamboat. In seconds the hacker was buried deep into the withy and I was squelching through the sticky mud to the water's edge.

The river was forty-yards wide with almost a quarter of a mile to the first bend, and up the centre of the river came Tom's steam-powered barge with a dumb-barge tied on each side. A dumb-barge was the name given to a narrow boat without engines. As the flotilla neared the pontoon moored outside our house Uncle Tom gave us the full benefit of the steam whistle that he had had customised, for he was a great showman in everything that he did. Uncle Tom bought the curlew and her dumb-barges alongside the pontoon and his bargees made them fast. As the big man stepped ashore he acknowledged my father and said to me 'did you see that boy, I pulled them alongside like stroking a cat, I really am the best boatman on this river,' and then he burst out laughing as he rubbed my head with his enormous hand.

When we arrived at the house mother already had cider, bread, cheese and raw onions on the kitchen table. She loved the visits from Tom, he always gave her a big hug and whispered something risqué in her ear that made her giggle like a schoolgirl. We all sat around the table together. That was the good thing about Uncle Tom, he always involved mum and me in his storytelling. He always started off in the same way by telling us how his family was and where he was going. On this trip Tom had left Birmingham

Opposite: Cutting willow in perch beds.

with a cargo of metal castings going to Sharpness for onward shipment to Ireland. He had then returned lightship to Gloucester and loaded sixty tons of animal feeds for Worcester.

Tom had hated the mud as a boy and much to my grandfather's disappointment had left this very house at fifteen years old to go to sea. He signed papers in Bristol on a Liverpool-based steam tramp as a 'peggy' (junior ordinary seaman) bound for Boston. This was such excitement for a boy who had, until then, been only as far as Gloucester accompanied by grandfather to deliver withies to the basket-makers.

Tom always joked that a Peggy was a rank even lower than that of a snake's wife. The duties were mostly cleaning officers' cabins, the wheelhouse and any other area prone to dust, dirt and fag ends. The most hated job was using the holystone. Large areas of the after decks of old steamers were wooden and these areas were scrubbed with water and a lump of pumice called a 'holystone' until a white pile appeared on the wooden planking. This was back-breaking work which almost guaranteed the loss of substantial amounts of skin from the knuckles and kneecaps. Although there was the excitement of world travel and the glimpse of foreign parts, with a ship only averaging a speed of eight knots boredom featured high among the hardships, especially for the younger men.

One of Tom's favourite stories was of the prank he had played on the stokers who were the biggest offenders of walking on his newly holystoned decks with coal-covered boots and dropping fag ends during smoke-o. On one particular ship there were large washrooms consisting of communal showers and washbasins with open grating below to enable waste water to run directly into the bilges. On the opposite bulkhead were situated eight sit-down toilets. They had half doors and a large wooden shelf sporting a cut-out hole for the necessary business. These toilets were reasonably comfortable due to the wide sit-on shelf and were frequented mostly by stokers for periods in excess of the time required for relief.

Under these boards was a galvanised trough which served to catch all the unmentionables. The trough had a slope of about twenty-five degrees and at the lowest end was a one-way flap that allowed the contents of the trough to go out to sea without allowing the sea to enter. At the top end of the trough was a seacock which, when opened, would allow seawater to enter the trough and wash all the unmentionables down and out to sea.

Uncle Tom would wait in one nearest to the seacock and at the top end of the gradient until the rest of the traps were full of stokers, then, barely able to contain his laughter, he would deposit a large bundle of newspapers rolled into a ball down his toilet, set fire to it, and open the seacock sending the fireball under the stokers one by one. Tom was fleet of foot and could escape into the bowels of the ship before the first bald-arsed stoker could rush screaming from the toilets.

I never tired of hearing Uncle Tom's stories, although sometimes he fell foul of repetition. A particular perennial of his was the South Atlantic shipwreck story. I would hang on his every word as he told how a voyage to Argentina resulted in him being washed up on a stony beach in the Falkland Islands surrounded by millions of penguins. He said 'I sat there shoulder to shoulder with the birds, trying my best to learn their language, until I was rescued by the villagers of Port Stanley.' Within two weeks the crew were picked up by a Norwegian whaler that had undertaken to give passage to the crew to Greenock.

Despite the smell of whale oil the Norwegian was a ship well-sailed by men from a master maritime nation. Tom had progressed, due to good reports from ships he had worked aboard, to the lofty rank of an able seaman thus being denied the pleasures of holystoning and was now standing his watch in the wheelhouse. Tom's berth on the ship was next to an old Nordic boatswain who prided himself on his command of the English language, which in fact was poor or Forest of Dean at best! His old face was like leather and he was missing one ear lobe and one side of his right nostril due to severe frostbite.

The whaler called at the Ascension Islands for fresh water and to report her progress to the owners through the good offices of Cable & Wireless who had a depot there. Some small amounts of food were chandled there, which included jars of blackberry preserve. They sailed the following day on the long run home and, as a treat, fresh bread and jam were placed on the mess room table for men between watches. Suddenly on sight of the jar the old boatswain leapt to his feet and, banging his huge fist on the table, he roared 'damn and blast, it take me fourteen years to say yam, now they change it to yelly!'

During the Norwegian whaler's laborious journey north she was, when in range, contacted by the owners to make for Dublin where some of her cargo of whalebone had been purchased by an Irish clothing manufacturer for the production of ladies corsets. Tom joked that he had asked to be put ashore with the whalebone and used as an inside piece. The whaler was berthed on the North Wall in Dublin and the agents for the company that owned the ship that had foundered in the Falklands were there to greet the crew.

The agent was there to give the choice to the crew to continue on to Greenock or to pay off there in Dublin. They stated that they would pay the wages due and arrange any paperwork required on behalf of the company. Most of the crew were Jocks and elected to continue on to Greenock for easy passage home. Uncle Tom and a shipmate from Barnstable called George Penley agreed to pay off the ship in Dublin, knowing that there was a high volume of sea traffic destined for southern ports in England. The following morning the two men said their farewells to their Nordic hosts and sought an official audience with the captain to thank him for their safe passage to Dublin.

George and Tom made their way along the quay to the agent's office, a Dickensian wood-panelled shipping office that smelled of leather, old books and cigar smoke. In one corner of the office on a raised dais sat a clerk with a tiny pair of glasses on the end of his nose and a small pinched mouth that seemed to be the result of his testicles being caught in a mousetrap and trying his best not to draw attention to the fact. Dead ahead was the portly carcass of the agent sitting on a worn leather Chesterfield smoking a particularly foul-smelling cigar.

He pushed some official looking documents across the table for the two men to sign. They were ships articles, and the signing of these papers meant that they were now officially signed off the ship that foundered in the South Atlantic and no longer the responsibility of the company. Orders had also been received from the company for the agent to sign the seamen's books with V.G.

There were three standards of report from the master when paying off a ship: V.G. (Very Good) G (Good) D.R. (Decline to report) V.G. meant that one could be almost guaranteed a berth at one's rank on any vessel of a recognised maritime nation. When the seamen's books had been signed the men were given a large brown envelope each with their name and the amount of wages they were to receive for their many months at sea: £95 15s 6d was a King's ransom to these men who usually paid off a ship with very little after drawing money against their wages to frequent drinking houses in foreign ports.

They bade farewell to the agent and the, by now, almost castrated office clerk and headed down the quay to the Flying Angel. The Mission to Seamen was referred to as the Flying Angel and was featured on their flag and on the wall of their buildings. It was set up by Christian charities to look after the welfare of foreign and domestic seafaring men. Most ports had one and their services were sometimes vital to seamen for shelter, food, spiritual comfort and some recreation, and any seaman on production of his sea book could avail himself of their comforts.

The missions were used as digs between voyages and to socialise with other seamen during long periods of cargo discharging in the port. The tariff for digs was 3d per night to include porridge in the morning, or was free if you were unable to pay. The rooms were small and contained six bunks; three on one wall and three on the opposite wall. The sheets were always clean but every mission seemed to have an uncanny ability of attracting the entire port's population of cockroaches. Tom said that the problem could be overcome by leaving a small bar of wet soap on the floor, which would cause the cockroaches to congregate around the soap whilst trying to devour it, thus keeping the insects off you. Tom's remedy was dual-purposed and could be just as effective if the soap were stepped on by an old salt returning from the pub, causing him to fall heavily in the darkness thus scattering the cockroaches to their daytime hideouts.

The young men's belief that a passage to the West Country would be easily obtained was well founded as the very next day they spotted a Bristol-based steam packet loading barrels of Guinness at the quay. The men moved along the dock as fast as the two helpings of mission-porridge would allow, as it weighed between one and three pounds per ladleful and was served up by an old peg-legged man with a large anchor tattooed on his arm, part of his ear having been lost to frostbite, with an inch-long candle of snot preparing itself for launch into your bowl!

The years and extreme weather conditions sometimes experienced in the Irish Sea had not been kind to this old ship. She looked sad and you could hear her plates groan as she bore the weight of each hoist of cargo that disappeared into her bowels. The mate was on deck supervising the stow. Tom caught his attention and explained their plight. After production of their seaman's books the old Bristolian welcomed them aboard. The old puffer sailed at 10.30a.m. and in two hours she was pushing hard into the teeth of a south-westerly gale. Unfazed she battled on through heavy seas that were pounding her starboard quarter and reducing her speed to just a few knots.

Tom had seen much bigger seas running in the southern oceans but

Old Bristolian coaster.

these were short, dirty and uncomfortable, depositing tons of seawater over her decks. At this stage they were still partially in the lee of the east coast of Ireland and they were all looking forward, with some trepidation, to the morning when the coast would no longer afford them any protection and the full force of the south-westerly would be on the starboard beam.

Due to the limited accommodation Tom and George were berthed in the chain locker, a cold dark storeroom in the forecastle of the ship used as a rope and paint store and to receive and store the anchor chain from the windlass above. Getting to the forecastle was out of the question in the weather conditions, so the men settled down in the corner of the wheelhouse to ride out the storm and swap yarns with the mate who was at the helm, chewing plug tobacco and periodically spitting the bitter juice out of the leeward wheelhouse window.

First light saw the old freighter still pushing south, but now without the benefit of any shelter from the Irish coast. However the gale had weakened and the seas breaking over her were white spray instead of the angry green of the night before. The old skipper had slept soundly through the night and the only reference made to the very severe weather conditions was 'bit dirty last night boys.' The average age of the four-man crew of this old coaster was without doubt sixty-five years, but these old Bristolians were indeed master mariners.

Tom had noted through the night that the old mate had hugged the Irish coast tightly, so that the vessel could be tacked easterly as soon as possible to avoid the full force of the gale directly on her beam. He had skilfully manoeuvred her to keep the seas on her stern as much as possible until they had rounded the Pembroke coast and headed north-easterly into the Bristol Channel with the benefit of a more comfortable following sea. These men thought nothing of this feat of seamanship and just considered the whole affair as a bit of a nuisance.

We were now making a handsome twelve knots and Lundy Island soon appeared off the starboard quarter. George trotted out his perennial joke 'if anything goes wrong I can swim home from here.' After an evening of telling old yarns they turned into their palatial accommodation in the forecastle chain locker, swinging in canvas hammocks that smelled of paint and sisal rope. The chain locker had one fundamental drawback; every time the old freighter rolled the anchor struck the outside of the hull which caused a sound similar to sleeping inside a large bass drum. As they journeyed further up the Bristol Channel the seas became kinder to them and the vessel rolled less with every mile they travelled, so that soon a deep sleep overcame them.

Tom did not hear the footsteps on the deck plates above and, without any warning, twenty tons of anchor chain began to rise up through the bulkhead over the windlass and through the bulwark into the sea. The noise of metal on metal was so loud that Uncle Tom swears that it affected his hearing so badly that ever since he has been unable to hear anyone in the pub say 'It's your round Tom.' After the huge pile of chain had reduced by half, covering as it went poor Tom in rust and dead seaweed from previous anchorages, the nightmare was finally over. With their ears ringing so loudly that nothing else was audible, the men gathered their traps and left the forecastle chain locker, moving down the ship towards the wheelhouse.

The old puffer was now lying at anchor off the island of Flat Holm, waiting for water to continue her journey to Avonmouth docks. Tom could see a wry smile on the faces of the skipper and old mate watching them from the wheelhouse windows as they made their way down the deck. 'What woke you so early?' called the mate, while a huge grin appeared on the skipper's face. 'Those bloody seagulls,' Tom replied, pointing to a flock circling the

The very wide lower reaches of the River Severn seen from Tidenham Chase.

ship. At this stage the four men broke out in uncontrollable laughter which continued until they reached the wheelhouse.

The basket was pulled up the mast to denote she was at anchor and all hands went below to a huge breakfast that had been prepared by a young seaman of about sixty years. These men had all been at sea for at least forty-five years and were now enjoying the coastal trade which allowed them to spend some time at home with their families whilst still being able to do the job they loved. They were indeed master mariners and Tom was aware that no navigational aids were used since they left Dublin other than a cursory glance at the binnacle and an old brass sea clock in the wheelhouse. All four men had served under sail in their youth and all wore the gold earring in their left ear. This ring was always placed in a young man's ear by his parents to ensure that there was enough gold to give the boy a decent burial in whatever country he was washed up. Some mothers even gave their wedding rings to be converted into earrings, and only gold was used, it being a universal currency.

At 10.00a.m. she heaved her anchor and followed the incoming tide to Avonmouth. The old steamer locked in with a large Dutch freighter, a local tug and three empty lighters for company. After locking up she slipped quietly onto her berth and the longshoremen made her fast. Within ten minutes all the crew had gathered their traps leaving only the engineer on board to close up. They made their way to the main gate of the docks and into the Royal Hotel, an infamous cider house frequented solely by stevedores and seafaring men.

Tom was first to the bar and set up pints of cider for all hands, and ale for George who had not drunk cider since throwing up violently into his mother's best hat at his sister's wedding reception when he was fourteen! Tom and George thanked the old mariners for their passage from Dublin and they laughed again at the anchor-chain prank from which Tom's ears were still ringing, before George walked the few steps across the road to Avonmouth railway station to start the last leg of his journey back to Barnstable. Tom walked with him and they said their farewells with all haste as the old tank engine bound for Temple Meads station was standing on the platform and about to leave.

Tom spent that night in the Flying Angel mission where his expert use of the wet soap had again kept the cockroaches away and almost succeeded in bringing down an old salt, saved only by the huge sea bag he was carrying which he managed to pull underneath himself before hitting the floor. He was on the lockside the next morning three hours before high water, knowing that small craft with shallow drafts would be first to lock out, and that some would be bound upriver to Sharpness. It was certain that he would know men on these craft, having lived his whole life on the riverbank.

Lined up like a row of ducklings waiting for the top lock gate to open was a Sharpness tug along with four lighters loaded with large trunks of aspen wood bound for Moreland's match factory in Gloucester, a narrow boat for Lydney and a grain barge loaded for the Tewkesbury flourmills that could take Uncle Tom right to his house on the riverbank. Tom knew most of the crews of these vessels, and all hands on the barge bound for Tewkesbury as he had been at school with most of them. They welcomed Tom onboard, and, after locking out and a short sail, they were soon swinging outside the piers at Sharpness.

With the fast run of tide it is necessary to swing outside the piers and head back into the tide to gain entry into the dock entrance without being swept past. The old barge locked in at Sharpness and headed north on the ship canal to Gloucester. She locked back into the River Severn and by late evening Tom was scrambling over the side onto our old pontoon. Tom never went deep sea again and worked the narrow boats from then on.

Tom had kept us entertained all evening around mother's kitchen table and at 9.00p.m. he took a pan of soup that mother had made back to the narrow boats to share with the bargees. Just after first light Uncle Tom again gave us the benefit of his customised steam whistle as the little flotilla moved slowly off our moorings. Soon the river would become too narrow to allow the boats to stay moored together and they would have to go in single file towed by the curlew, meaning that they would all have to steer their own narrow boats with hand signals, their only form of communication.

CHAPTER FIVE

A PLATE OF ELVERS

The end of March and the beginning of April meant very little sleep for father and me and turned us almost nocturnal for several weeks. Into the Severn, Wye, Parrot and some rivers in Ireland had arrived the elvers, one of nature's finest feats of survival and reproduction not to mention a great source of protein and enjoyment to river dwellers. The tension could be felt in all the pubs, churches and Sunday schools in anticipation of the first sighting of these tiny eels.

My grandfather always said that river families had no children born to them around the Christmas period due to all the men spending every night elver fishing on the river in March. Father had an uncanny ability of determining the arrival of the millions of these long-awaited tiny creatures that were hell-bent on the upper reaches of the river. 'They're coming, I can smell um,' he would say. But it was the fact that he knew exactly when the big tides would push the elvers up the rivers, and when the weather conditions, the state of the moon and of the winds were right that was so incredible. All this was learned from many generations of river-dwelling.

The elver has a seven-year cycle that begins in the Sargasso Sea off the coast of America, a dirty green sea partially covered in weed and a 'bit creepy' so Uncle Tom always said, having sailed through it many times. The eggs of the eel hatch in their millions and the tiny elvers are swept north by the Gulf Stream drift and into the rivers in the south-west of England. Predation of these tiny eels on their way across the Atlantic is enormous and only a small percentage of the creatures arrive in our rivers. However the elvers still arrive in their millions and are now perfectly formed eels, about the size of a darning needle. They are almost transparent with a thin grey line down their centre, the perfect time for them to be eaten.

After a few weeks the elver's grey central line turns black. They make their way into the pills, small streams and ponds, sometimes even squirming through wet grass to gain access to a particular pond or stretch of water. At this stage they are called bootlaces and start to devour everything from carrion to tadpoles, weed and grubs in their struggle to grow large enough in six years to swim back to the Sargasso Sea to start the seven year cycle all over again.

At the first sighting of the clouds of elvers it was every man for his tump. These were grassy pieces of bank that protruded into the river and made

Old Mr Brown elvering on the Wye from a cherished tump in Llandogo in 1963.

The beautiful River Wye on a summer's day at Redbrook.

Tidal lower reaches of the River Wye taken from Wintuor's Leap, 2009.

the use of the heavy elvering nets much easier. Father had his own way of constructing his elver nets but there were many different forms and variations depending on where you lived. Nets downriver from Gloucester were of a different construction, as were those used on the Wye and Parrot, but they all looked similar and did the same job.

Except for the netting which was a coarse gauze made by the old cider maker's wife, the nets would last many seasons, but it was inevitable that some had to be replaced from time to time. We would cut a nut stick about as thick as your wrist and eight-feet long, when it was just sprouting leaves and was supple and full of sap. It was then split down the middle for about three feet and whipped with strong twine to prevent it splitting any further. The split sides were then bent into a Y-shape and a spar placed in the mouth to keep it open. Two split willow sticks were attached to the front spar running down to the joint of the Y. They were bowed and lined with the gauze to create a net. Before the netting was fitted we would dry the wooden frame in the chimneybreast to keep its shape.

'Get the kit ready, we should see some tonight,' father would say. The kit, which would have to be carried to his favourite tump, depended on the size of the tide and several other mystical reasons known only to father and contrived to make me work as hard as possible. There were the nets, buckets, metal crooks for holding the carbide lamps, carbide in a waterproof bag and finally two flagons of cider. Elvers seemed only to be catchable on

night tides and travelled deep down in the river on daytime tides. This is a mystery that not even my grandfather had the answer for, and my theory was that they wanted to keep people up all night as a reward for their attempts to eat them!

High water was at 2.00a.m. and at midnight the incoming tide would begin to stop the flow of the river; it was time to start dipping the nets. It was a most attractive sight to see the carbide lamps from other rivermen twinkling on the water as they too worked their own tumps to reap this bountiful harvest. On a good tide each dip of the net could produce two or three pounds of elvers from the surface of the river, which were tipped into the waiting buckets. It was a cold wet job but in a way quite exciting, and, as usual, there was a laugh to be had. One dark night we had caught well and had all that was needed for the next day's deliveries. Dad sent me back with the full buckets to tip into a firkin that was on the back of our cart ready for the next day's deliveries and to return with a treacle tin that he had left in the shed.

Elvering three hundred yards upstream from us and in our perch beds was Will Palmer, a miserable man with a sense of humour akin to that of Attila the Hun. We moved slowly through the willows until we were directly behind old Will. Dad had made a small hole in the bottom of the treacle tin with his knife and had removed the lid and placed a small amount of carbide, elvers and mud in the tin. Carbide and water gives off

The art of elver fishing.

a highly inflammable gas that powered our lamps, but if compressed it becomes very explosive. We carefully placed the tin on a mound of turf directly behind Will. Dad put a cupped handful of water in the tin to activate the carbide, and then jammed the lid on as tightly as possible. While the lethal brew began to fizz and bubble he attached a small length of sisal twine to the hole in the base of the tin and again adjusted his aim towards the unsuspecting victim.

The sisal twine was ignited, knowing that it would smoulder only slowly, allowing our escape from the scene of the crime. We made our way with all haste back towards our cottage. Halfway back there was an enormous explosion and a flash in the dark sky, followed by a loud scream and a just-audible string of obscenities drifting down the now-silent riverbank. We heard in the village the next day that Will Palmer had been blown up by some gypsy kids and festooned in mud and dead elvers!

Elver-selling day was the day that I most enjoyed of the many and varied jobs undertaken by the river hobbler. I had placed the night before's catch in a nine-gallon open-topped firkin on the back of the cart, and as soon as I had hitched Jenny up we were off for the day selling. The day had already started well because mum had not called me until 8.00a.m. instead of our customary 5.30a.m., and we had all eaten a large breakfast of eggs and home-cured bacon, enjoying a good laugh about our explosive prank the night before.

We would start at the villages furthest away from home and work our way back in the evening. Father had a hand bell, and as I eased Jenny through the villages he would ring it as loud as he could, at the same time imitating a cockney barrow boy, and in a London accent shout things like 'lovely live elvers, come and get um, only 3d a pint, roll-up roll-up!' Over the years everyone had come to instantly recognize dad's Gloucestershire-Cockney selling techniques, and waited with their chipped enamel bowls to purchase these much sought-after delicacies. On the side of the elver barrel hung a pint beer mug and this was the measure for 3d-worth. 'Keep yer 'and over um Mrs or they ull be gone, and that ull be a threepenny Joey mam, thank you.' People only wanted fresh live elvers and they all knew that ours were caught only a few hours before, although they did not know about the explosive demolition of Will Palmer's elvering coat!

Due to the murder and butchery on the Somme and in Flanders there were many fatherless homes in the villages, and some of the women and children were at starvation level. Father was mindful of this and if we had some elvers leftover he would go out of his way to take a feed to widowed women that he knew were struggling particularly hard to bring up their children with only the aid of odd jobs and handouts from the church. He would jump off the cart and take a pint to the families that he knew could not afford them but were too proud to ask.

Outside pubs were our best selling-places but I had to constantly remind father that we were here to make money and not to spend it! After a full day and evening of selling we could earn up to £4 10s, a large sum of money for us. We would get home at about 10.00p.m. after having a great many laughs, no hard work, and a large sum of money as well as doing some good for struggling families in the villages. This routine of catching one night and selling the next day and evening would continue until the run of elvers was over, approximately three weeks with some breaks when the tides were not right or there was too much fresh water coming down the river from heavy rains further up.

Elver cooking and eating was again different on various stretches of the rivers. Some boiled and pressed the elvers into a 'cheese', which they later cut into slices and fried; we only ate elvers live and thrown into a pan with hot bacon fat, followed sharply by a firm lid before they made their escape.

We had a large garden with a pigsty at the bottom under the overhanging branches of a big elm. Every year it was occupied by a different pig, fattened and killed by father to provide for all the meat requirements of the house. A rinnock would be given to dad in exchange for anything he could barter,

Long netting at Newnham-on-Severn.

and sometimes for nothing. A rinnock – or runt – is a small weak piglet from a large litter that, unless given special treatment, would die and was therefore uneconomical to keep for a farmer or pig breeder.

We would take the piglet home and mum would bottle-feed it until it was strong enough to live in the sty on its own. It would be fed almost entirely on house scraps and soon put on weight. Every pig, regardless of its sex, was called General Haig, after the man my mother blamed for callously sending so many young men to their certain deaths, including mother's two brothers at Flanders and other battlefields. This was to remind mother to stop her from getting too attached to the pig when it came time for us to kill it.

When the time came father would straddle the pig between his legs, pull its head back by the snout and cut its throat from one ear to the other. After some horrific squealing the pig would bleed to death and fall to the ground. We would then roll it onto a bed of straw and set fire to it to burn off the whiskers, soak it with water and scrape the burned whiskers off, leaving the pig bald and pink. Father would butcher the pig wasting nothing, and one of his favourite sayings was 'the only thing I don't use from the pig is its squeal.' The curing was mum's job and in the scullery she had a salting stone that must have weighed five cwt. The real art of good bacon and ham was in the curing, and mother was an expert.

She fried the bacon in a large pan until it was so crispy that all the fat had left the rashers, she then removed the rashers from the pan and into the fat she tossed the live elvers that would turn white on impact with the hot fat. The elvers were cooked for just a few minutes until they began to turn brown, they were then removed from the pan and reunited with the bacon and eaten without delay. We had a feed of elvers for lunch or supper every day while the season lasted.

CHAPTER SIX

BELOVED PANSY HANCOCK

Joshua Hancock was the owner of a small fleet of narrow boats working mostly in the Midland canals area. The fleet consisted of six horse-drawn narrow boats used mostly in the Birmingham area, and one over-powered steam boat with the ability to be accompanied by two dumb barges which he used for long-hauling and river work. Josh was a regular visitor to our family home for the past thirty years, and a great friend of my grandfather, father and Uncle Tom.

Joshua was born on a narrow boat and spent all of his life travelling the rivers and canals of Britain with his wife and daughter Pansy. Like many other families they spent their entire lives in a single cabin that measured fourteen feet by six feet, and in the summer months they slept on deck or in the hold under the tarpaulin covering the cargo. Pansy steered one of the dumb barges and Mrs Hancock the other, but most times the boats were lashed together, with Joshua at the helm of the powered narrow boat in the centre. This allowed the women to cook, clean and launder. Other families franchised the remainder of Hancock's narrow boats and a rent was paid for the boats and horses.

Father and Uncle Tom were living at our house with my grandparents. Father was newly married and Tom had returned from his seafaring exploits and rekindled his relationship with Pansy who had been his childhood sweetheart. The Hancocks came alongside our pontoon about once a week for rabbits, cider, and any other supplies Joshua could barter for with my grandfather. Hay was also loaded at our pontoon for shipment to Birmingham to feed the barge horses. Uncle Tom joined the Hancocks in the business when Josh and his wife bought and moved into a house in Stourport, which they hated for a long time, but the move made sense in view of their advancing years.

Tom and Pansy were married in what was quite an upmarket ceremony at Worcester. They say that about fifty narrow boats – all decorated with flowers – were berthed in the river beside the cathedral, and that children were washed clean of coal dust and cursing was kept to an absolute minimum. Pansy was a beautiful girl but she was strong-willed and had a temper that could be explosive. She would not tolerate injustice and always championed the cause of fair play. Tom loved her dearly but she could be a handful, although I think this was one of the qualities he admired in her.

One time the couple were in Avonmouth loading tinned pineapple bound for the British Waterways depot in Birmingham. They had one dumb barge in tow, which was the maximum that they could tow in the fast-running tide of the River Severn. During the loading of the cargo Tom decided he would go to the pub outside the dock gates to see if any of his shipmates were ashore having a drink. Pansy said that she would sheet the cargo and make ready for sea but that he must be back by 4.00p.m. for the first lock out of small boats which they would have to make to have enough water to lock in at Sharpness. He was also under strict instruction not to get drunk as they all knew the lower reaches of the Severn does not suffer fools or drunks easily.

At 5.30p.m. Tom and an old matelot pal from his deep-sea days came stumbling down the quayside, singing and patting each other on the back and telling one another what thoroughly good chaps they were. The boats had been loading from a large freighter on X-berth that had recently arrived from east Africa. Tom said his fond farewells to his pal at the foot of the gang plank of an old Newcastle collier and continued along the quay in the direction of the large red and black freighter that his boats were alongside when he departed for the pub.

After peering through one eye at a time to lessen the chance of an increase in his fleet of fifty per cent, some large gulps of air and much pulling of the forelocks, Tom decided the boats were no longer where he had left them. A conversation carried on with a stevedore, for Tom's part conducted mostly in Swahili or some kind of cider-drinking language, revealed that Pansy had moved off the berth at 4.00p.m.

Avonmouth was a very busy port and was crammed with vessels of all sizes waiting their turn to load or discharge cargoes from all around the globe. Tom dragged his inebriated body up and down the quays, stumbling over bow ropes and walking under ship's cranes in a now desperate search for his wife and his craft. Tom's search was ended by an off-duty lock-keeper who informed him that, contrary to all the advice from the lock-keepers, Pansy had sailed at 4.30p.m. for Sharpness, unaccompanied, with the fully laden boats.

Pansy's knowledge of the Severn estuary was good, but only very experienced men attempted the task ahead of her and even then with some trepidation, as one misjudgement of tide, wrong location of rocks, or sandbanks would almost inevitably end in disaster. Mechanical breakdown in these treacherous currents while unaccompanied, and the sheer under-power of the craft also posed a deadly threat. Nevertheless Pansy rounded the north pier of Avonmouth dock entrance and headed on the first leg of her journey, a straight course to Chapel Rock and the Beachley Point, both visible about five miles ahead.

She had lashed the dumb barge to the port side of her craft, and with strong following tide she made good time crossing the wide expanse of

Avonmouth roads and was soon at the Chapel Rock. From hereon things became very much more difficult. In her enthusiasm to cross the wide expanse of the estuary and gain station on the opposite bank she had steamed too fast and reached Beachley two hours before high water at Sharpness, and so stood a good chance of going aground through lack of water. She must have looked tremendous standing on the after end of the steam barge with her arm and waist holding the tiller at a 10 per cent angle to compensate for the strong run of tide and the influence of the barge tied alongside, her long hair blowing out in front of her from the following south-westerly wind.

Pansy eased down enough to keep steerage, for if the speed of the tide is greater than the speed of the propellers it means no control and the inevitable destination would be rocks, sand bars and, when in the upper reaches of the river, pushed by flood water it could result in being in the living room of some poor fisherman's cottage. The little craft hugged the Welsh bank of the ever-narrowing Severn, still slightly ahead of time and now entering the most difficult and demanding part of the journey Pansy had noticed that something was going seriously wrong. The lashings holding the two craft together had become slack causing the hulls to collide heavily with every movement.

Pansy was about to turn to starboard to cross the river again to the English bank and the Shepperdine Light in particular. She knew that this would put her beam to the tide and bring the small craft tightly together, so she decided to wait until she had lined up the light and started her heading across the river. When the heading was set and the craft were closely alongside she moved carefully along the narrow walkway at the side of the boat with a skein of rope around her neck knowing that one slip would mean almost certain drowning.

She reached the forward deck cleats and over-lashed knowing that she could not slacken and reuse the existing lashing without the two craft being forced apart. She used a figure of eight lashing that her father had taught her when she was a small child, and after securing the fore end she moved back along the edge of the boat, trying not to look down at the tide of brown sandy water ripping between the two small craft. After carrying out the same procedure on the after-end lashings Pansy moved back into the boat and, after a dramatic course adjustment, headed on towards the Shepperdine light.

This was not a straight course and included a dogleg through the sand bars which was negotiated in daylight by marks used on the shoreline. Some used Oldbury-on-Severn church, others used the Windbound Inn, it depended on the means handed down from father to son. The light was fading as the little craft reached the channel on the Sharpness side of the river and turned to starboard and headed for the dock piers. Her timing was now well adjusted and she would be at the piers at one hour before high water. With most of the power still in the tide, she knew that she would have to swing at the piers and head into the tide to enable her to enter the piers without being washed past, which she knew would happen if she tried to enter with the run of the tide behind her.

As darkness fell, Pansy swung the narrow boats outside the piers and under full steam peeled off into the outer basin and safety . The locks were lowering a small tug and a Dutch coaster, and when the lock gates opened and they cleared the basin, Pansy steered the boats gently into the lock. A lock gate-keeper threw down a line and Pansy made the craft fast to the lock wall. 'Where's Tom then Pansy?' asked the harbour master when he came to collect information regarding the destination of the boats and the cargo they were carrying. 'Avonmouth,' she replied. 'How'd you get 'ere then Pansy?' he asked. 'I sailed,' she replied, and he walked away in disbelief.

When the lock was level and the gates were opened she moved into the dock and berthed at the first available space, then, with a dip bucket, set about washing the salt and sand from the small boats as her husband always did, to stop the corrosion. Only when she had swilled down all the affected areas with fresh water from the dock did she go below for a wash and to warm up the stew she had prepared during the loading at Avonmouth.

After she had eaten and cleared away she lay on her bunk and a deep sleep crept over the exhausted woman, which did not release its grip until 5.30a.m. the following morning. With all haste she washed in a pail of cold water and made ready to leave the dock and start her journey up the Gloucester ship canal, knowing that the first bridge at Purton would open for her at 6.30a.m.

The canal was wide enough to enable the two craft to remain coupled for the entire passage to Gloucester, a trip that Pansy had taken hundreds of times since being born on a narrow boat in the canal at the Patch Bridge at Slimbridge, helped into the world by the landlady of the Tudor Arms and a bargee's wife. At every bridge that she passed through and on every other craft she met someone would pose the same question; 'Where is Tom this morning, having a lie in is he?' She would acknowledge the person, but answer the question with a false laugh or a silly little joke to gloss over the real reasons, not wanting to lie, as her exploits would be the talk of the waterways by the end of the week.

At Saul Junction her close friend Rose Smith was opening the bridge for her husband who was at a crucial stage of onion planting. She pushed open the heavy bridge often because her lazy husband was always at the 'crucial' stage of something that stopped him doing proper work. 'Ow are you darlin' and 'ow's that lovely man of yours?' Knowing that only Rose was within earshot, Pansy let go some of her pent-up anger and frustration, 'The bastard's still pissed up in Avonmouth I think,' and as the small craft slipped through the open bridge, Rose was left standing to attention with her bottom jaw now resting on her ample bosom.

Pansy steamed on with the sun at her back and her long hair gently blowing in the breeze. She pushed the tiller mostly with her hips because her hands, which she had now bound with rag, were badly blistered and bleeding from her struggles with the savage tides of the Severn estuary the day before. Late morning found the boats in the Hempsted straight heading for Llanthony Bridge and the docks just beyond. As she eased down, waiting for the bridge-keeper to open the final bridge of her canal passage, she recognized the handsome and imposing figure of her husband standing alone on the bridge ahead of her.

He was as she had left him; dressed in corduroy trousers, a coloured shirt and the bright red neckerchief that he always wore. She could also see the large gold earring his mother had sent him to sea with. As she came nearer the tears began to roll down her cheeks, due in part to total exhaustion, the severe pain in her hands and the realization of the danger she had exposed herself to on her epic voyage through the treacherous Severn Estuary. But most of all due to the sight of the man she loved more than any other thing in the whole world.

As the little barge and its narrow boat slipped through the bridge Tom was standing on the side of the quay. Pansy hurled every word of foul language she knew, and also some she did not know the meaning of but that she knew must be very bad because she had heard the stevedores on Bristol docks using them. She did not move over to allow Tom to board but carried on through the docks to an empty berth at the far end. She made the boats fast and went below, leaving Tom to walk the length of the quay.

The big man went into the accommodation to find Pansy sitting on their bunk changing the blood-soaked rags that bound her hands, shaking uncontrollably from the exhaustion and fear that she had held back for the entire voyage. Tom gently lifted the girl up by the armpits and held her close. He could feel her heart pounding, like having a small bird in this hand. He kissed her tenderly on the cheek and lips and with her tiny hand in his he began to clean her wounds with warm water and coal tar soap. The love that radiated from the girl's eyes and through Tom's tender loving hands to her filled the ragged little ship with a love experienced by only a few.

After Tom had been marooned in darkest Avonmouth he had caught the train to Bristol and another to Gloucester. He was almost paralysed with fear knowing the mighty feat required by his wife to reach Sharpness alone with

Pansy Hancock.

under-powered craft fit really only for canal work. He kept on telling himself that the tides were good, it was daylight and that Pansy knew more than any other women he knew about the estuary and the effort it was going to take to reach her destination.

The train had arrived at Gloucester at 9.15p.m. and Tom ran without stopping from the station to the harbour master's office. He knew it would be manned by someone he would know well enough to telegraph their opposite number at Sharpness to confirm the whereabouts of Pansy and the boats. 'She's just locked in here and moved on to the coal berth for the night,' came the reply. 'Bloody hell, she was on her own then?' came the next response from the shocked and totally confused Sharpness lock-keeper. If the harbour master had not been in his office Tom would have cried with relief and pride for the extraordinary demonstration of skill and bravery the girl had shown. In the coming weeks Tom told every man, woman and child from Bridgewater to Nottingham and Llangollen to London about the legend created by his beautiful wife, but the only mention he ever made of it to her was, 'you did well girl.'

At daybreak the following morning the boats locked out of the docks and back into the river again, this time with Tom standing firmly at the tiller and Pansy sat beside him on an empty wooden cider crate holding the big man's hand with her right one, a large mug of tea in her left. They would be in Birmingham by tomorrow night to discharge the cases of pineapples at the British waterways depot as if nothing had happened. Three months after Pansy's epic journey she gave birth to their first child at her mother's house at Stourport.

CHAPTER SEVEN

SALMON, SHAD AND SIMPLE NUNK

The elvers have gone now and it is time for the majestic salmon and the lowly shad to dominate our lives on the riverbank. There are many names for the salmon, again depending on where one lived along the rivers, the time of year and the age of the fish. There are also many ways to catch them and prepare them for eating.

It was May and father and I were sharing our time between perch-cutting for the basket-makers and salmon fishing for the big house and anywhere else we could sell them. A large fishmonger in Gloucester would buy from us as many as we could supply, but we would have to have them at his yard by five in the morning for him to pack them in boxes and cover them in straw and ice for their train journey to London. The words used when talking of salmon in the local pubs by rivermen left some of the visitors to the big house questioning whether they had been cast adrift on some foreign shore where the inhabitants spoke only Swahili or Forest of Dean.

Such words were used as, hoop nets, stop boat, putchers, lave nets and gaffs when referring to the means of capture of this fine beast. In our methods of fishing there was never any mention of Devon minnows, bloody butchers or expensive Sage fly fishing rods as used by fat old ladies somewhere on the River Spey in Scotland, whilst being supported by a small army of hairy kilt-clad ghillies laden down with basket loads of cucumber sandwiches dearly wishing that the old cows had stayed in London. Words such as snots, botchers, cocks, hens, and cypes were all used in explaining the age and condition of the fish.

Early one morning at the end of April, father and I had gone lave-net fishing at low water in the sand-bank pools left by the falling tide. Lave-net fishing was easy but getting the equipment down the banks and two hundred-yards out into the river was hard going. The lave net is a heavy Y-shaped wooden frame, with net placed over the Y-shape to trap the salmon and a long wooden shaft to carry and operate the net; the whole thing weighed about twenty pounds. To reach the sandbanks the shaft of the net would be placed on your shoulder with the net hanging over your back and the walking would start.

First wet silt, sometimes three-foot deep, would have to be waded through to get down the bank to the water's edge. Fast-flowing water that runs close to the banks would then have to be waded through until we could reach

Above: Alfie Smith with two nice salmon at Apperley, c.1950.

Right: Lave-net fishing and salmon putching.

the high and dry sandbanks and the pools we required for the fishing. On our arrival at the riverbank I tied up the horse and cart to a large piece of driftwood that had been deposited on the goose grass by a previous high tide, and as we began to unload the nets we heard the plaintive cry of Nunk Deacon running and stumbling along the bank.

Nunk was the size of a small church spire with the mental age of about six. He walked very fast and was bent forward, which gave the appearance that his mother had pushed him out of the house in the small of the back and he was having trouble stopping. His shoulders were always well forward of his body and his hands hung loosely by his sides. His coat was buttoned up to his neck and his corduroy trousers stopped about four inches above the tops of his boots.

My father was a hard man but he was always mindful of the less fortunate and had a soft spot for Nunk. As Nunk approached, the permanent grin he wore spread wider across his face until it reached each ear, exposing teeth that

Lave-net fishing and salmon putching.

strongly resembled those belonging to a two–man crosscut saw. As he arrived he pointed first to the lave nets, then to the sandbanks, then to himself and back to the sand banks again, prompting father to say, 'wonna come fishin' Nunk?' Whereupon he kicked off his unlaced boots and jumped off the grass bank into silt up to his knees, waving to us to follow him into the mud. After sliding and squelching through the mud we reached the fast-flowing waters between the mud and the sandbanks and dad made Nunk stop and hold on to the shaft of the lave net while we crossed to the dry sand.

The first two pools had fish trapped in them; the larger pool had two and the smaller had one stranded fish in it. Father gave his net to Nunk and told him to catch the fish in the small pool while he had a pipe of tobacco. Nunk ran towards the pool and began to chase the fish around with the half submerged net; his laughter could be heard from Gloucester to Sharpness. Suddenly the fish turned and slammed into the back of the net. The look of excitement on the boy's face as he felt the weight of the silver beauty hit the net made father cough his pipe out into a puddle.

With one giant heave Nunk raised the net and the large salmon out of the water. He must have been holding forty pounds at arms length while he ran out of the pool towards father. He dropped the net, fish and all, at father's feet, then, with a huge smile, he began to point first to the fish then to himself then back to the fish. After a quick ruffle of Nunk's hair, father despatched the twenty-pound cock fish with a wooden priest with one clean hit to the back of the salmon's head. We knew the fishing would be good as the tides were at their best. Soon we had all the fish we could carry from the pools and started back to shore long before the tide began to run in. When we were pool-fishing on the exposed sandbanks the tide would be watched very carefully, because to be cut off by the fast incoming tide would mean certain death.

When we reached the fast-running water between the sand and the silt of the bank it was still running out, but sometimes we had left it so late that the tide was starting to turn. Some without father's skill had left it later than that and had paid the price with their lives. We had netted about twelve fish, one hen about twenty-six pounds, a mixture of cocks and hens of about twelve pounds and a botcher of about six pounds; that is a lot of weight – with the nets as well – to carry up through the silt to the cart.

Father had given Nunk a length of hessian cord and told him to feed it through the fishes mouths and out of their gills, tie some fish around his waist and hang the twenty-pounder he had caught over his shoulder. After an exhausting wade through the fast-running water and a half wade, half crawl through the thick Severn silt, we finally reached the goose grass bank and old Jenny and the cart. With great relief we began to unburden ourselves of the nets and fish into the cart. At that moment father noticed that Nunk was only carrying the fish he had hung over his shoulder. 'Where's the rest of the fish I told you to hang around your waist?' asked father. 'I still got um,' he replied, and opened his baggy corduroy trousers to reveal four salmon hanging from the hessian rope inside his trousers.

After scraping the worst of the mud from our clothes, we set off across the flat goose grass. Father sat on the shafts and Nunk and I sat on the back of the cart with our feet hanging down. Three hours' consumption of lush green grass had given Jenny flatulence of explosive proportions which she relieved with every movement of her hind legs. 'Bloody horse could fart for England,' we heard dad mutter under his breath. We were all covered with mud but there was a sense of euphoria from the fishing trip and the enjoyment we had derived from Nunk's antics as we left river road and turned into the village.

Our first stop was at the Plough Inn where father jumped from the shafts of the cart and hit the ground running, driven by the irresistible urge to inflict further damage on his liver with several pints of scrumpy. Nunk pulled Jenny up onto the village green just outside the pub where she could consume ever more lush grass. We sat on the pub steps and before long father appeared with two pints of cider shandy and told us he would not be long, though when I was younger I had sat for many hours on pub steps all over the West Country. I was outside today because Nunk was with us and dad would face the wrath of his mother if he took him into the pub.

Next-door to the pub lived Miss Cox. She was a nasty, mean old spinster and when kids kicked a ball over her fence from the village green she would stab it with a kitchen knife and throw it back. This had gained her the name of 'Splitter Cox, public enemy number one,' and fair game for village pranks. As Nunk and I sat on the pub steps, Splitter Cox came out of her front gate. She was wearing her normal widow's weeds; black lace-up boots, a shawl round her shoulders, a willow bread-basket over her left arm and a hat that looked like the *Mayflower* in full sail. Uncle Tom said that she had a face like a smacked arse and a nose like a blind cobbler's thumb and that was what she was using today. As she shuffled off in the opposite direction I knew that she had not seen us and a dastardly plan began to form in my (bored with sitting outside the pub) mind.

I went to the cart knowing that dad kept an old rusty tin of tools against the tailboard and I took out a lump hammer and a rusty six-inch nail, with Nunk primed as lookout. I drove the nail through the thick gate and into the gate post. I drove the nail deep and rubbed some mud onto the head to prevent its detection by the old crone. By this time Nunk was so excited that he pointed first at the gate then at me, then back again to the gate. I put my finger up to my mouth to signal that he should not let on what we had done, so he pulled his old top coat over his head in the firm belief that if he could see no one, no one could see him. He skipped and stumbled behind me to the cart where we dumped the hammer and then ran to sit back on the pub steps; his smile was as wide as the Severn.

Spring flowers had gone now. There were still some tulips left but daffs and crocuses lay spent and sad from their great spring effort. One open and flagging tulip looked like a red shiny satin dress I had seen in a draper's shop in Gloucester. Mother passed the dress by with barely a glance; what was the good of torment when the reality of owning such a garment was as remote as a day without toil. I was always fascinated by flowers and I was totally engrossed in the pub flower border when my coat sleeve was almost pulled off by Nunk.

He was pointing down the road and using the same trusted format as before, his overcoat was covering his entire head to avoid detection – the crone was returning! We were both seized by sheer terror as we leapt into the cart and laid flat on the floor peeping through the cracks in the tailboard. Nunk was still in ostrich mode and my chin was resting on a slimy twenty-pound cock salmon. Splitter lifted the latch on the heavy gate and I could almost hear her dirty black talons scrape over the top spar as the gate refused to budge. It was at about this time that my arse reduced itself to the size of a small green pea as I lay shivering in the cart.

Splitter was now shaking the gate so violently that the posts were beginning to loosen in the ground. After making every effort, which included the driving of her huge hips and bottom into the gate, she began to look around, suspecting foul play. Our death now became a distinct possibility and was saved only by the return of father to the cart. Seeing us lying prostrate in the cart he suspected mischief and so pulled Jenny up quickly from the grass and moved her off up the lane. The horse knew when dad meant business, and with a large section of the trumpet resonating from her bottom we moved briskly up the lane, all the time putting distance between us and the furious crone. Normally my father was dead against any mischief or disrespect towards women or older people, but as a boy he had also suffered at the hands of Splitter Cox and I could hear him giggle as I told him the tale.

Nunk's mother was scrubbing the front step of the cottage as we pulled up at his gate. The boy, now with his head fully exposed, was clutching the twenty-pounder under one arm and pointing first to the fish, then to father, then to himself and all the time trying to tell his mother of the adventures he had had during the day. 'Bless you Lionel,' Mrs Deacon said to father. Dad knew that the fish would be a welcome addition to her food supply. He also knew that the boy loved to go with us and that she was thanking him for his kindness. Her husband had also been a victim of the not-so-Great War that had murdered half the young men in the river villages.

CHAPTER EIGHT

BIG BULLS AND CARROTS

Father had picked up a small job in the pub for the next day, which would still leave us time to net some shad in the afternoon. Hobbs Farm had lost their bull, bogged down and drowned in a steep rhine. This had left the farm with no bull to service the milking cows that were the major source of revenue for the farm. We were to walk a bull from Home Farm the two miles to Hobbs Farm, where Julie had a cow and heifer that were bulling and needed to be serviced. We were at Home Farm bullpen at 7.30 the following morning to collect Westland Monarch, a huge Hereford-Frisian cross that was the biggest bull I had ever seen.

Dad spoke to the cowman who gave him the bull pole which was used to walk the bull, the only way the monster could be controlled. The pole was between eight-foot and ten-foot long and had a spring-loaded hook at one end that was placed through the large ring in the animal's nose. Twisting in one or the other direction would determine the animal's course, pulling on the pole would control the speed of the forward motion, and finally and most importantly, pushing the pole back would prevent the beast from charging forward. I have left out one most important tool; 'mind over matter.' Unless the animal knows that you are in charge and would stand for no nonsense the other techniques I have mentioned would be to no avail, and the best result would be a change or two of corduroy trousers, the worst a visit to Gloucester Royal Infirmary!

We moved slowly through the village and out into lanes leading to Hobbs Farm. The man who ran the local pub that I had spent so many happy hours sitting outside the previous day was a Taff from up some dark satanic Welsh mining valley, renowned for silicosis, rickets and allotments surrounded by large sheets of corrugated iron. He had left the valley under some sort of cloud, probably he had a nephew who once played rugby league or some other great crime against the Welsh nation, and had moved in with the widow at the pub. He got his feet further and further under the table over time and was soon referred to by the men in the village as the cock-lodger. There was always good-hearted banter between him and the locals, mostly about vegetable growing, and as we walked along the lane father told me of Taff's latest story of vegetable propagation.

Someone at the bar had been rash enough to mention the size of his carrots last year when Taff rounded on him. 'Talk to me about carrots boy-o is it,' he said, 'do you know the reason I left the valleys?' Everyone stopped what they were doing, waiting for the answer to years of gossip and speculation. 'Carrots,' he said, 'the carrots in my allotment one year had grown so large and long isn't it, that the pit ponies were eating the bottoms of them, which forced me to leave my allotment, my wife and the valley!' There was a deathly silence for some seconds then the whole pub burst into uncontrollable laughter. With a huge grin on his face Taff's next comment was, 'beat them carrots you bumpkins.'

Julie met us on our arrival at Hobbs Farm. She had confined the cow and heifer in the yard and was awaiting our arrival. She moved a gate to one side and we lead the leviathan into the yard. The cattle were bellowing loudly from being separated from the rest of the herd and by now the old bull had begun to turn up his top lip at the smell of the in-season cattle. 'That cow been bulling for two days now, I hope she's not gone over,' said Julie. Father and I moved out of the yard as the bull became more and more excited with the prospect. Julie had removed the pole from the bull's nose ring and watched his advancement on the cows with interest.

'Bulling' was the term always used for cattle that had come into season and required servicing to produce the next calf and the next lactation period for the production of milk. The bull with its top lip curled back had made his first lunge at the cow, but she would not stand and the huge bull was forced to crash back to the ground. The second attempt was more successful and the old cow strode for him but he could not engage. In a flash Julie was under the bull and with two tons of rampant bull above her, she took a firm hold of the bull's massive penis and guided him in. She moved quickly out from under the bull as he penetrated the cow, and moving behind him she lifted up his tail and with a riding crop she lashed the bull across the back of his legs to include part of his scrotum, which heightened the animal's arousal but did nothing to stoke my enthusiasm for the rapidly approaching village hall dance. The procedure was repeated until the cow and heifer had been serviced and let out of the yard to join the rest of the herd. 'Not many girls would go under a mounting bull,' said Dad 'no wonder they rate her so highly as a cowgirl.'

While the old bull was given time to settle, the Mrs of the house came out with two mugs of tea and a pair of bacon sandwiches, made up of about two pounds of home-cured bacon crisped up and still with whiskers on the rind, spread thick with butter, all enclosed in two enormous snowls of homemade bread. Julie passed the time of day with dad and talked about her stock, the loss of her beloved bull and the well-being of her mother and father.

Bacon sandwiches devoured, Julie went back into the yard, put the pole back in the bull's nose ring and lead him out of the yard as meek as a lamb. She was fearless where cattle were concerned and had such a gift of putting them at their ease. She said her farewells to father and me, and as we started off with dad at the pole and me at the rear of the bull she grabbed my arm, turned to me, and with fire in her eyes said under her breath, 'I'll see you at the dance next month.' I instantly experienced extreme pain in the back of my scrotum as I meekly submitted to her demands.

Westland Monarch safely returned to the Home Farm bullpen we headed for home. No money ever changed hands for jobs like these but this meant that there was one in! A favour, a credit, and this would not be forgotten when a bag of spuds was needed, or a bag of mangles for the pig, or a cord or two of timber.

CHAPTER NINE

FISHCAKES AND
MAVIS STOKES

We collected from our shed a throw out net, a hoop net, and a clean nine-gallon firkin, placed them all in the cart and headed up the river to find the shad, a miserable fish of the herring family. Tasteless, bony, and a pain in the arse when you were salmon fishing with nets because sometimes there were so many they would fill them up in seconds. I could never tell the difference but there were supposedly two types; one called the Atlantic shad and one the Allis shad. Again there were local names for the creatures, Twait and May fish being the most widely used.

One day on the riverbank a naturalist-type fellow, all hair, teeth and wellington boots, unable to pronounce his R's (which seems to be obligatory for all naturalists), began to tell father and me about the amazing lifestyle of the shad. He told us how the shad belonged to the herring family, and had the ability to change from salt to fresh water, and spawned in the upper reaches of only the Severn, Wye and Usk rivers. These facts had been known to us for generations and father's only question was 'did he know why the Lord had not sent them up French rivers instead?'

An hour up the river got us to one of dad's favourite elvering tumps. 'The water's black with the bloody things,' he said, and with about four shoots of the throw out we had twenty pounds of fish. The throw out is a net that has floats on the top and small weights on the bottom, and is thrown across the river to entangle anything passing. We fished for about an hour, dad throwing and me clearing the net of the catch, which was not easy as the fish have large fins and are difficult to untangle from the net. Dad called time on the whole operation when the firkin was two-thirds full. We dunked the nets in clean water, swung them round to dry and put everything back on the cart for the journey home.

Mother knew we would not fail her and had the copper boiling when we arrived home. The only thought I had was how to escape the stench that would permeate the wash-house and surrounding area for the next few hours. My Uncle Tom had brought home from Japan the sharpest knife I had ever seen for mother to use for fish gutting; it was so sharp I had seen my father shave his face with it. She used this knife with the dexterity of a concert pianist and could head, tail and gut fish so fast her hands were a blur.

Guts went in a bucket for dad's eel traps and the fish into the big wood-fired copper that she had lit some hours before and that was now

The River Wye from Wintour's Leap.

bubbling like some giant witch's cauldron. Fish were followed into the copper by salt, pepper, handfuls of bay leaves and a secret mixture of herbs she had collected and chopped earlier. This selection of herbs was a closely guarded secret that mum said was given to her mother by a gypsy women on her way to the strawberry fields at Cheddar. After the water was brought back to the boil, the fire under the copper was completely extinguished leaving the contents to steep until cold.

We spent most of our lives fishing, eeling, elvering, or trout tickling but neither dad nor I could stand the smell of mum boiling the May fish, despite the net result being so delicious and sought-after all over the county. The fresh south-westerly had by now dispersed the smell of boiled fish, which allowed me to resume normal breathing and dad to reappear from the shed wiping cider from his moustache. 'A lie-in tomorrow, pig castrating at Home Farm,' was his only comment.

Mum had made breakfast and was boiling fifty pounds of spuds in the copper after removing the cold fish when dad and I started for Home Farm, dad sharpening his pocket-knife on a smooth flat stone he carried in his pocket as we walked on through what was turning into a beautiful spring day. Home Farm kept about one hundred pigs split between, Gloucester Old Spots and Wessex Saddlebacks as porkers, Landrace and Tamworth as baconers. They all ran outside and being ring-less they would plough fifteen acres in a season, which left the land fertilized and aerated for proper ploughing in the autumn, which was usually followed by a planting of spuds the following year.

Mavis Stokes joined Mother in the task of removing all the bones and skin from the cooked May fish. Mavis – now there's a woman for you! Since I was born I had never seen her without a baby or small child breastfeeding from her. Anyone under the age of about twelve was likely to be subjected to this mothering. The slightest sadness or sorrow, loss of toy, skinned knee or even hesitance at entering the school gates due to expectation of bullying was accepted justification. She had five children from her husband who died on the orders of some jumped-up general with a name like Olay Ponsonby Biscuit Barrel III in order to gain about two yards of mud in Belgium; someone should have told those bastards we had plenty of mud in the Severn.

Mavis was loved by everyone in the village and her bizarre behaviour was brought about by a genuine need to couch and cuddle any child in distress. As a young boy I was afforded this luxury more than once. I can remember taking a heavy fall from the back of dad's cart one day when I was about six years old. The pain was excruciating and skin hung from my kneecap in tatters. Gripped by pain and fear I sobbed uncontrollably until a large arm raised me from the gravel and, in a well-practised move, clothing was pulled to one side and I was coupled to a large, warm and mum-smelling bosom.

The tight wrappings from her shawl endorsed the sense of warmth, comfort and security. A slow rocking motion and the humming of some mystical tune completed the whole treatment. The whole thing lasted about five minutes, by which time we had reached the local shop, when my lips were gently prised off leaving a large ring of dirt, grit and snot around her bosom. I was gently lowered to the floor. She dried my tears with the end of her shawl, licked her hand and flattened my hair gesturing to my dad that I was alright now. The lady in the shop gave me a teaspoonful of sherbet wrapped in a twist of paper and Mavis kissed me on the head as we left the shop, mended and totally at ease.

Mum and Mavis sat on kitchen chairs stripping every last piece of flesh from the fish, leaving no skin or bone whatsoever. The potatoes were then cooked, drained and cooled in the old copper to a temperature that was just bearable to the touch. To the potatoes was added two large blocks of home-made butter, the fish, dried parsley and mum's special mixture of herbs known only to her and half the gypsies of Europe. The mixture was mashed and the consistency constantly adjusted by the adding of milk until it was perfect for moulding into cakes the size of the palm of your hand. Stale loaves of bread had been dried and turned into breadcrumbs and the fishcakes were egged and rolled in them until they were evenly covered and the process was complete.

Laid out on trays and separated with sheets of greaseproof paper the fishcakes were now ready for distribution; fifty to the village shop, fifty for the cook at the big house. These were cash-money jobs and mother was so pleased with her 'little bit of money,' as she called it. Mavis would have as many as she needed to feed her brood and a feed would be dropped off at Nunk's mother's, which was always gratefully received. Mum would never tell what Mavis and she had spoken about, but they would laugh the whole day through and most of the next day too. Dad would say to me that it was 'woman's talk' but I suspected that it was dirty jokes and light-hearted gossip.

Mum's efforts had ensured a wonderful day out in Gloucester the next day to deliver the bulk of her fishcakes and a large box of salmon we had netted from our boat the day before. It promised to be a very good day, as mum would receive cash for her fishcakes and it was payout time for all the fish we had supplied to the monger throughout the season.

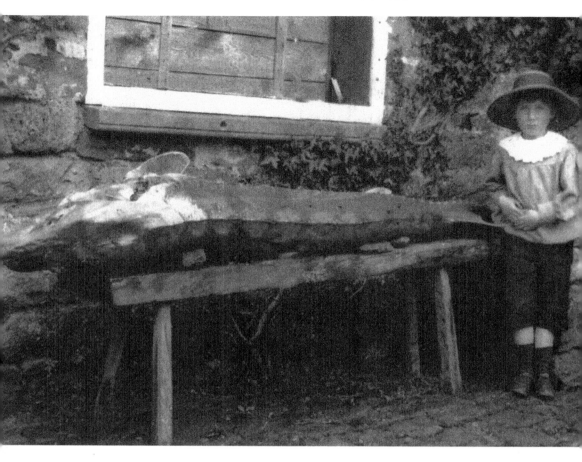

Much the largest of British freshwater fishes is the Royal sturegon (Acipenser sturio). The heaviest recorded specimen was one weighing 392lb and measuring 9ft 2in long, which was taken in the River Wye at Llandogo, Monmouthshire, in June 1877.

CHAPTER TEN

PIGS AND PARTIES

We arrived at Home Farm, dad's knife now honed to perfection, the task of pig castration about to begin. About thirty piglets had been enclosed in a small sheep-pen all hand-picked for castration. On our arrival the estate manager Toby Williams, a large man in tweed plus fours and jacket topped by a silk cravat and flat cap, warmly greeted us. Dad was the only man - including his lordship - that I ever heard call him Toby to his face, and this was because of the high esteem in which he held my father. He would have loved father to be his under manager but dad was a riverman and loved the liberty and diversity that this gave him.

Placed outside the pen was a bucket of warm water, turned milky by the addition of some Jeyes Fluid, a bundle of clean rags and a large bottle of undiluted Jeyes Fluid. Mr Williams was carrying the key piece of equipment, two very large wellington boots that had a heavy brick inside each foot. I had assisted in this crude large-scale vasectomy many times and knew my role by heart. We gathered the equipment around us and set to work.

My role was catcher and washer, but before any start could be made a dry square of rag was ripped off, soaked in spit and jammed as far into one's ears as possible. Dad said that the noise from thirty small bore pigs losing their manhood was louder than the guns opening up in the evening at Passchendaele. Now it could begin. I would catch the piglet by the back legs, drop him headfirst into the wellington boot and place my legs both sides of the boot to hold it steady while I washed the pigs scrotum area with the wet rag dipped in the diluted Jeyes Fluid mixture. The dexterity with which father and I handed the wellington from leg to leg was like an emperor penguin handing over her egg whilst trying to keep it up off the ice.

Dad's skills were now brought to bear and he would slice open the scrotum with his super-sharp knife, and with his thumb and forefinger he would squeeze out the testicle and nip it off with the knife at exactly the right place. He poured neat Jeyes Fluid into the scrotum cavity, tipped the pig out of the Wellington boot and so on until all the piglets had been done. On release the animals would perform forward somersaults, many revolutions of the sheep-pen whilst squealing so loudly they could be heard up in the Cotswolds.

Incidentally, after being a part of this surgical nightmare, my own testicles could be located somewhere between my shoulder blades and the back of my neck, and my scrotum had disappeared completely. The post-operative

Squeals and wellies.

care consisted of dad returning four days later and kicking any piglet that was not moving to see if they had gone stiff with the lockjaw, but the success rate with father was nearly always one hundred per cent and this was why all the farmers used us.

Mr Williams was again very pleased with our work which had saved large veterinary bills and lost not one pig to lockjaw, and in turn this would mean one or two rinnock piglets for dad, enough straw for winter bedding and all the timber we would need for firewood for the whole winter. The whole operation had taken about two and half hours.

The back-kitchen of the big house was the place to be at this time of day and Mr Williams was heading us straight for it. The smell of freshly baked bread and other delights was overwhelming. The kitchen was very large with a black-leaded range and huge ovens on either side. There were so many cooking utensils; butter churns, salting stones and some equipment I had never seen before. Pheasants, rabbits, ducks and hams hung in the cold pantry next-door and every shelf bore butter, cheese, pastries and preserves in plenty.

Mr Williams left us in the kitchens with Mrs Brown and we sat down at the huge scrubbed table that would seat about ten on each side; it had been crafted by my grandfather from oak grown on the estate. Mrs Brown and father were great friends and had known each other all their lives. As it was still only about 11.00a.m. we were plied with hot bread and freshly churned butter, large lumps of brawn in jelly, pickled cabbage, onions and a very large mug of tea.

Time had come for the village fête and the dance in the village hall that I had been looking forward to throughout the summer. I eagerly anticipated my promised liaison with the wonderful Julie Illes, although the experience with the bull still gave me a feeling of apprehension. The thought of holding Julie would override any fear I held of being abused in a similar fashion as the poor beast for not performing to her satisfaction. The weather was perfect and the fête was the largest we had ever had, with lots of sideshows, food stalls and a huge marquee housing the flower show and cooking competitions. The whole village was here, including the master of the big house and his wife, who were judging some of the competitions.

The vicar, in black spats and a straw hat, was slowly becoming inebriated in the beer tent, and by 1.00p.m. had to be rescued by his wife who was wearing a hat that strongly resembled an upside down piss pot with a feather in it. Gwen, always a good sport, who had breast-fed everyone under the age of fourteen, had volunteered to sit in the stocks with Nunk who went into uncontrollable laughter every time he was hit in the face by a bundle of wet rags or some rotten fruit. Julie was there with her parents and she looked stunning in a printed dress, no shoes and a simple flower woven into her hair. She was certainly the most healthy, tanned example of a girl I had ever seen.

I met up with a mate that I was at school with and we headed for the beer tent with the intention of getting in the right frame of mind and gaining some bravado to face the challenges of the dance and all that it promised. Three pints of cider later we were, like all young men, starving hungry and full of mischief. The pie-making competition had been judged and undoubtedly won again for about the fortieth year by Splitter Cox who always took the pies back home instead of leaving them to be sold for the church funds. The back of the large marquee was at the end of the beer tent and it was easy to pull out a tent peg, sliding under and into the show tent.

I slid under the canvas head-first and was confronted by a pair of old lady's shoes topped with baggy thick stockings, but, fortunately, the top half of my body was obscured from the woman's vision by the display tables. I stayed frozen to the spot until the wearer of the thick, baggy, light-brown stockings had moved off. The judging of the cookery had been carried out and we knew our goal was a pie with a red card placed by it: it was bound to be Splitter's. The tent was now unoccupied as the judges had moved to the flower exhibits for their final judging.

We crawled through the table legs to where the pies were and there, in all its majesty, was the winning pie with its red card proudly displayed. Like a limbo dancer I snaked up and lifted the pie leaving the red card on the table. We weaved our way back through the table legs to the point of our escape, slid under the tent and into the gap between the beer tent and the tent that had been the scene of the crime.

This was the best Blaisdon plum tart I had ever tasted and we greedily ripped the pie into large lumps which we devoured, barely taking time to chew. The pleasure was greater knowing that we were eating Splitter Cox's prize-winning pastry. Two more pints of cider and ten minutes of wobbly, giggly walking later and the prize-winning pie went into reverse and was jettisoned, along with most of the cider at the foot of a large chestnut tree at the edge of the show field. 'Ah well,' dad said, 'young men need to have too much cider and throw up occasionally because it gets the badness out of them!'

I bade farewell to my partner in crime, who still looked rather green and wobbly, and I headed for home knowing that I needed a lie-down and take time to recover before I slicked up for the dance in the evening at the village hall. I was just washing in the sink before going to lie down on my bed when I heard Jenny being reined in outside the house. When the horse had stopped farting I could hear my mother laughing at the top of her voice and more excited than I had ever heard her before. She burst through the door holding onto dad's arm. Across the kitchen she came, and throwing her arms around me she said 'first time in anyone's lifetime I beat Splitter and won first prize with my Blaisdon plum tart.' Oh bollocks! I never did tell mum but she would not have cared because she had the red card that said first prize.

Mum had ironed my shirt and trousers. I was washed and spruced up and had 5/6d in my pocket, more than enough money for my beer and the 6d for my entry ticket to the dance. I had had a haircut yesterday morning at Twiddley's. Twiddley was the local barber and worked from a converted cylindrical gypsy caravan parked on the edge of the village green under an old ash tree. The beds had been removed from the caravan and some seats

placed around the walls, which were always occupied by old men from the village talking and sometimes arguing about every topic imaginable. The caravan smelled of stale brilliantine and the walls were covered in pictures of champion boxers wearing huge ornamental belts around their waists.

Twiddley was a short man who always wore a striped shirt with no collar attached and a black serge waistcoat. As a young boy I lived in mortal dread of Twiddley's wagon and had to be dragged kicking and screaming by my father to receive a painful basin-shaped haircut. However, now I had become a young man the prospect of a haircut was not so daunting, and sometimes it could be quite interesting listening to the old men discussing various subjects. In later years I heard the first mention of a man called Adolf Hitler who, one old sage was convinced, would plunge us into war against the Huns once more.

Outside the village hall I met another river hobbler's apprentice like me who had ridden his father's bike all the way from Framilode. We talked about the year in general and he, like me, was looking forward to the arrival of thousands of winter visiting geese which represented good money for us and a great deal of fun. The vicar's wife was on the door taking the entrance fee and was still resplendent in the upturned piss pot hat she had worn at the fête. We paid our dues and sheepishly walked to the nearest seat we could find.

Julie was with some friends and was making out that she had not noticed me but I know she had watched me walk across the hall and was now whispering to her mates. Cider was the answer to these shyness problems and I asked my pal to get them in and I would pay if I did not have to suffer the embarrassment of walking across the dance floor in front of Julie and the other girls. The music was to be supplied by an accordionist, a drummer and a fiddle player with bad acne, but for the time being it was a wind-up gramophone manufactured by someone called His Master's Voice and operated by the vicar's daughter. She was an unfortunate-looking spinster with teeth that protruded out so far that she could have eaten an apple through a chain-link fence. She also had a concave chest and a miserable disposition.

Boldness had not yet become my companion, despite two pints of rough cider, when Julie came over and asked, 'are you going to speak to me or dance or do something?' I stammered something incomprehensible and before I could take stock I was up and mixed into some sort of a barn dance or Gay Gordons. Although I was very fleet of foot, a dancer I was not! However, with Julie holding my hand, and no one else quite knowing what had to be danced, I got by and had fun. The most important thing though, the ice was broken! We danced, talked and kissed as much as would have been proper with the vicar's wife at the door and most of the parish in the hall.

How could we get outside together past all the prying eyes and without putting the village's morality at risk? At the rear of the hall was a room where cups and plates were stored, where the Women's Institute had their meetings and where the parish council decided on things like whether the roadman should be sacked for always being drunk. On the back wall of this room was a small window that led to the back of the churchyard. While our mates supplied cover we slipped through the door and into the meeting room.

I pulled a chair up to the window, opened it and was out within a flash. Julie followed head first and I held her close as I lifted her from the window. As I held her I ran my hands over her beautiful body. We sat in the graveyard for many hours kissing and holding each other. I unfastened the buttons on her blouse, but with my hands shaking with excitement I could not undo the tiny buttons on her liberty bodice. With great dexterity she unfastened each small button and pulled the garment open. The moon was shining on her and I knew then she would be the woman with whom I would spend the rest of my life.

CHAPTER ELEVEN

GANDERS AND CIDER APPLES

It was late autumn now, a season of fruitfulness, wet legs and the return of the proverbial mud. Jenny hated the autumn. It meant a wet back and a lot of hard work apple hauling. Although the old horse worked every day, she was more a means of transport to us and really had no hard work to do. But this was apple hauling time and she would be put to the test with a full cart every trip.

Most of the cider fruit we picked up and hauled went to the press in the village, run by a man called Raindrop Cooper, who would press for a third and top-quality fruit for a quarter. This meant he would press everyone's fruit and keep one third of the juice as payment which he would make into cider and sell to pubs and the public on a commercial basis. However, if the fruit was of a superior variety, say Kingston Blacks, he would only charge a quarter of the juice for the pressing.

Some fruit we would take to Mr Illes but he mostly purchased and hauled his own, and pressed fruit only for his business. Most of the village women earned some pocket money apple picking up. It was hard, backbreaking work as they moved from orchard to orchard. Most fruit that was picked up included a generous helping of fag ends, fox shit and leaves, which was all very acceptable and flavour-enhancing, rendered harmless by the same acids and alcohol responsible for the destruction of half the livers in Gloucestershire.

Brook Farm had about fifty mixed cider-fruit trees which ensured enough cider for the regular farm hands plus the casual labour brought in for haymaking and thrashing. We arrived at the farm where most of the fruit had already been picked up and the sacks stacked against the trunks. At the far end of the orchard a small gang of women were still picking up, bent double with their bottoms in the air. We loaded as many sacks as old Jenny could comfortably haul and headed for the women to tell them we would be back for the remaining fruit.

Mrs Pullin, a lady with an ample bottom, was in charge of the gang and she had a sharp sense of humour. Dad drew Jenny up close to Mrs Pullin, and with the exertion of the load being hauled, Jenny let rip with the loudest and longest fart that I had ever heard. 'Pardon me Lionel,' Mrs Pullin said, 'we 'ad pickled onions up the farm.' The women all went into uncontrollable laughter and Jenny let rip again!

The cider mill was a ramshackle affair, fraught with the dangers of exposed pulleys, belts, apple grinders and a hundred other moving parts, poised to claim the careless and unsuspecting limb. The mill had an earth floor and was as well lit as a Forest of Dean coal mine. Nevertheless, it had served Raindrop and his father before him and had made the villagers' cider for many years with the loss of only one hand from Raindrop's entire dynasty.

As we unloaded the fruit the sacks were tipped into a hopper by Raindrop's Neanderthal nephew called Walter, who was capable of picking up a bag of apples weighing at least one hundred pounds in one hand but who was a total stranger to the English language or handkerchiefs, and was always the proud owner of a four-inch candle of snot which sometimes must have found its way into the cider.

In the engine house next to the mill room Raindrop was busy stoking the stationary steam engine with logs. By the throwing of a lever known only to him and his ancestors, the belts that gained entry through holes knocked in the wall began to strain and whip, and pulley wheels of all sizes sprang into action resulting in the operating of the apple grinder. Ah, the apple grinder, a fiendish piece of equipment which consisted of a series of spikes and blades on rollers which cut and smashed the fruit into small mushy pieces called slurry.

The rollers were encased in a wooden frame and fed with fruit via a hopper at one side and relieved of its slurry by a chute at the other, all driven by a belt and flywheel mechanism from a further unguarded pulley above. As the machine sprang into action Walter was tipping apples into the hopper and looking into the grinder. Due to the fact that there was too much fruit in the grinder before its start up, it had a blow back and Walter's head was instantly festooned in slurry to the thickness of at least one inch.

Raindrop reappeared from the engine house and began to place the first hessian sheet on the bottom board of the cider press and awaited the first wheelbarrow full of the apple slurry that Walter had drained from the grinder. 'I told you not to put too many apples in the grinder before she started up didn't I?' said Raindrop, as he watched Walter advancing with the barrow. But he knew his advice would go unheeded, and Walter wiped the slurry from his eyes with the sleeve of his old brown smock. He was barely aware of the rest of his upper torso being covered in mashed cider fruit.

The first mat was filled with the slurry, folded into an envelope and a thin board placed on top. This procedure was repeated until the press was full to the top board which was attached to a greasy worm and gearing mechanism, driven again by a series of belts and pulleys, controlled by a kind of clutch lever. As pressure was brought to bear by the lowering of the top board, the apple juice would run through the hessian envelopes, down the sides of the press and into a large barrel sunk in the floor underneath. This means of juice extraction had been used for many years and dad said he had seen long-stalked straw used in northern France to make the envelopes instead of hessian.

When the press was lifted, the crushed apple slurry was called apple musk, and was piled up outside to be used for animal feed during the winter months. The juice was pumped with an old hand pump into the waiting empty barrels, belonging to the customer, and the pressing share pumped into Raindrop's large hogsheads which were racked up along the back wall. In some places a man's standing in the village was measured by the quality of his cider barrels, which greatly influenced the taste of the product.

New barrels were not treated with much respect and beer barrels were only just acceptable if they were over five years old and had been used for a good dark beer. Malt whiskey gave a wonderful taste to the cider and was ranked highly, but the Rolls Royce of barrels were those that had begun life as French brandy containers. Men would kill to have a hogshead with French writing on it, let alone the word 'cognac.'

I can remember Uncle Tom coming alongside our jetty with some barrels stacked on his hatch covers that men had purchased from an importer at Bristol. Well, it was like a national bank holiday. Crowds lined the riverbank and grown men giggled like children, for it was the Martell brandy barrels that had arrived! With apple hauling finished, cider made and racked up, the destruction of the West Country's remaining healthy livers was assured for another season.

Julie had asked me if I would help her to drive some cattle to a special market for prime animals that was being held in Gloucester. She had asked me months ago and I was looking forward to a day out with her, away from the prying eyes of the old women in the village, who still thought it a sin to walk through the village holding hands while unchaperoned! We were not busy on the river for it was too early for the wild fowling, and father could manage emptying the eel wheels and the re-baiting on his own.

I was at Hobbs Farm at 5.00a.m. on Saturday morning and Julie had mustered four of the finest beasts I had ever seen. Two pedigree Holstein heifers and two Holstein Hereford cross bullocks. The animals had all been scrubbed, combed and even their hooves were filed and polished. These were prize-winners and a credit to Julie and her expertise as a stockman. What is more, they would make top money at the sale after the showing.

The bullocks had bulldog clips in their noses and could be easily led on a short rope. Castration takes all the aggression out of a bull calf and allows them to fatten more quickly into the fine bullocks we were now walking to market. The heifers would walk nicely on their own, as long as they were not spooked by something. Julie had a great calming influence on all cattle and seemed to speak their language, reassuring them as we went.

The nine-mile walk seemed nothing to us and we stopped and kissed many times in the lanes. I even tried my luck again at the old liberty bodice buttons, but this frontal assault was soon brought to a halt by Julie, and the appearance of an old man on a bicycle with a face like leather and a nose like a blind cobbler's thumb. It was a beautiful autumn morning and the trees were adorned with dew-filled cobwebs that glowed with all the colours of the rainbow as the morning sun shone through them. Life was really good, being in love and a river hobbler.

We drove the cattle into market without any trouble and they were penned by the auctioneer's men, bullocks in one pen and the heifers in another. 'Good stock,' one of the men said to Julie. 'I think you'll get a rosette today.' There was two hours to go before the judging, so with a cursory glance at the opposition's animals we made our way to a shed that served as a canteen for the market workers, stockmen and farmers. The smell of cooking bacon was overwhelming. I had money, 7s 9d in total, which was a lot because I had saved for today by cutting down on my beer drinking with my mates and sold some point of lay fowls that I had reared myself.

'Two bacon sandwiches please, and two mugs of tea.' I asked. The lady behind the counter had an arse that strongly resembled that of a dray horse used by Whitbread and it was clear she was no stranger to the odd bacon sandwich herself. When the deal was done the counter groaned under the weight of the sandwiches that must have contained a pound of bacon in each and a large loaf between the two. In Gloucestershire a thick slice of bread usually accompanied by cheese was referred to as a 'snowl.' We sat on a bench outside the canteen and dismantled our bacon sandwiches, as there was no way our mouths would open wide enough to accommodate a pound of bacon and four inches of bread. We sat and made small talk, held hands when no one was passing and had such a good time. It was like being on holiday, not that we had ever had one.

As we ate, Hezekiah Williams, who people said was in his nineties but no one - including him - knew for sure how old he was, came up to Julie and said 'they bullocks of yours are the best I sin yer today and are a credit to ee.' This was praise indeed from such an old sage and expert in livestock as Hezekiah. The old man farmed a smallholding adjoining the farm that Julie worked on and he had kept a keen eye on the stock she was rearing. Hezekiah used a walking stick made from a bull's penis with the thick end let into the forked prong of a deer's antler. He wore hobnailed boots and thick leather gaiters, a battered trilby and a genuine nineteenth-century milking smock that even had the crosses embroidered on the breast plate. It was said that he started every day, summer or winter, at 5.00a.m. with two pints of rough cider and three raw eggs.

The bullocks won best in the show and the heifers had a second and went on to make top money at the auction. We had a good walk around the

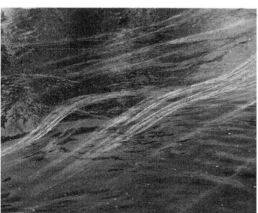

Wildlife abounds on the banks of the River Severn.

town, a good laugh and a bag of chips. We took the charabanc back to the village, which was a rare treat as bus riding was usually reserved for Sunday school outings.

With the first of the frosts came the beautiful skeins of geese heading south from the artic to winter in warmer climes, such as ours. I always marvelled at the sight of the long skeins on a frosty evening silhouetted against the bright orange of the evening sun and the low honking sounds they made as they glided onto the wetlands beside the river. Any romantic notions of this miraculous migration were however soon dispelled by the thoughts of the food and cash-money this abundance of feathered meat would bring to the river people at this lean time of year.

They came in their thousands, sometimes in their hundreds of thousands; Canada, Pink-foot, Greylag and Barnacle geese. Day after day they came, food and money for us, but misery for the local farmers as they took the last available grazing from the sheep and covered the ground in an inch of acidic goose shit, rendering the field useless for any further grazing that year.

Tumps had been formed in the wet meadows most frequented by generations of river men. These were earth mounds, hollowed out over the years and used to lie behind and rest the duck guns on. They were mostly downwind of the geese and this allowed for a clear shot to most of the field. Chapped lips and chilblains were the reward for lying hour after hour behind the tumps, which were sometimes half full of water, waiting for the flocks to arrive each night. If I complained dad would say, 'ah well, every cloud has a silver lining,' referring to, I think, the silver under the belly of the geese. A mixed metaphor if ever I heard one!

A small boy would be hidden in the hedge close to the landing site with strict instructions not to make a sound, while the men lay still behind the tump that the geese would be allowed to land on and start to graze. The kill rate was much higher if the fowls were flapping two feet above the ground trying to take off from a standing start. So they were allowed to settle before the boy would bang a tin and shout, causing a thousand birds to try to take off at once. While they were flapping just above the ground the guns would open up on them, inflicting many casualties on the flock.

This was a grizzly business and not for the faint-hearted, as many birds would be wounded and flapping wildly, trying to escape with broken wings and legs. We would run into the mutilated flock, catching the wounded ones first, cutting their throats with pen knives to let them bleed which made the meat less dark. All sorts of guns were used, from twelve-bores to old black powder blunderbusses, filled with ball bearings and bits of metal swarf. During the day we would pluck and dress the geese, ready to take to the same man in Gloucester market who took our fish and elvers. By evening it would all start again.

Father and I did a lot of duck shooting as well at this time of year, but this was done on the river itself, on our Severn punt. One night in November, at the height of the moon and with a heavy frost on the ground, the river five hundred yards upstream from our jetty was almost full, bank to bank, with mallard, teal and some shell duck. They could be seen gathered in small huddles on the calm, moonlit water. It was a good night for wildfowling, but very difficult to get in range without being seen.

To walk the banks where you would be silhouetted against the bright moonlight was impossible, and would guarantee putting the fowls to flight. The only way to get close enough to achieve a worthwhile kill rate was by punt. Ducks would take no notice of a punt slowly and silently gliding towards them. It could be a large log or a crocodile, or a fat drunk person having fallen from Haw Bridge, but whatever it may be ducks do not look for danger coming at them from the river.

I had just walked home from the pub and had noticed the large flocks of wild fowl; I also suspected a long, hard night as I knew father would not miss this opportunity. Yes, as I came to the riverbank at the back of the house there was father leaning over the Severn punt, loading guns and sacks in the bright moonlight. 'Get some old gear on boy, we got work,' he said. Our punt had a duck-gun stump three feet back from the bow. This was a four-by-four piece of timber which extended through the bottom of the punt and had a 'V' cut into the top to lash a duck gun to.

The wildfowler would lie in the bottom of the punt with the butt of the gun against his shoulder and the barrel lashed to the stump. There was a very strong recoil from a black powder duck gun which could not be absorbed by the shoulder without being lashed to the stump. The loading of the gun was critical and far too technical for a young man like me. Father used to say, 'I think you have to be an octogenarian to load that gun!' Though I was plenty old enough to paddle the bloody boat the whole length of Gloucestershire and incur blisters the size of small mushrooms from the age of fourteen!

The gun was loaded with lead shot from dismantled twelve-bore cartridges, small nuts and bolts, and ball bearings if you had any, as well as some black powder and wadding. This was a highly dangerous practice and could result in the breech not being able to stand the charge, but this is how my grandfather had done it and his father before him, and if all went well the kill rate was enormous. A double-barrelled twelve-bore was also taken, loaded with cartridges of number five shot, which is larger than would be used for other game. Three shots, one from the duck gun and both barrels of the shotgun, were all you would be able to get off unless you wanted to spend all night on the river waiting for the fowl to return after the first salvo.

All the guns were loaded, the big one lashed to the firing stump. One improvised landing net for retrieving dead ducks from the water and two large hessian sacks for the spoils. We carefully slid the punt down the bank and into the water. Father took up position, lying in the bottom of the punt and looking down the barrel of the duck gun. I pushed us off and sat as low as possible in the stern end, sculling with a short handled paddle. Sculling is a method of paddling over the stern and not down the beams of the boat, where it could be seen. The paddle never comes out of the water and is just twisted from side to side to propel and steer the punt without any noise at all and only minimum movement by the boatman. This was one of the most skilful arts of a riverman and had taken me most of my young life to perfect, as it is difficult to teach and can only be perfected through the feeling in your hands and years of practice.

We slowly headed for the middle of the river which was about one hundred and fifty yards wide, flat, calm and with very little fresh water running down because we had had quite a dry autumn. This made for less blisters on the paddler's hands, as it was easier to go upstream if the flow was less. We made steady and silent headway toward the flocks of fowl, breathing into our overcoats so as not to show streams of hot breath that could scare them into a premature departure while still out of range.

The modus operandi was to get about forty yards from the flock, not too close for the shot to chew the birds. I would sit up and fire one barrel of the shotgun over father's head and into the floating flock, and as they rose from the water and were at their most vulnerable, father would open up with Big Bertha and I would fire off the second barrel of the twelve-bore. This is how it always was and, father said, 'always would be', and thank God it was years after his death that some naturalists, most with speech impediments and wooden toggles on their jackets, opened the Wildfowl Trust and took part of our lives away, along with thousands of years of tradition.

The transportation part had gone well and my first shot into the flock had bagged about five birds – then disaster! Father had fired at the rising birds, but he had loaded too much black powder into Big Bertha. Her breech held, thank God, but the recoil ripped the gun stump out of our ageing Severn punt and the gun and stump were catapulted into the air and over the side, while a four-inch fountain of water began filling the boat at an alarming rate. Within a few minutes we were rendered amphibious, seventy-five yards from the bank and in twenty feet of freezing water. All father could say was, 'save the duck gun and the twelve-bore.'

An old Severn punt being used to evacuate women and children from the Coalhouse Inn at Apperley during heavy flooding in the 1960s.

The old duck gun was still afloat, lashed to the wooden gun stump, so with the twelve bore down my trousers I swam, pushing the duck gun and gun stump in front of me until I reached the home-side bank. Father, without a backward glance, was heading down the bank towards home. We had been in the water through various adventures more times than I care to mention and this is why father treated it without any concern, knowing that I would be alright and, more importantly, that the guns were safe.

As I reached the house with the heavy guns, father had on some dry clothes and was heading for our other small rowing boat, shouting at me to hurry. 'No time for me to change then?' I asked. 'You'll be alright boy, we got fowl to collect.' I was perishing cold as father rowed out to the ducks, which had by this time floated almost downriver to the house. With father's expert rowing of the boat, we soon collected all the dead fowl and then started to search along the banks for the wounded ones. When Father was satisfied, and I was on the point of hypothermia, we headed for our jetty. A total of eighteen ducks had been collected, mostly mallards, but at the cost of our one-hundred-year-old Severn punt, which we never did try to recover, and soon after father fashioned a new one.

CHAPTER TWELVE

A SAILOR'S LIFE
FOR ME

Once again the bleak midwinter is upon us; nothing much to do. A bit of rabbiting, barrel cleaning and the eel wheels were still catching in the rhines and streams which gave us a bit of cash-money, but all in all things were tough going at this time of year. Favours were called in for work carried out in the busy times; a load of logs here and a free run at the potato bury there, some straw for the pigsty and anything that was going to help us through this lean time.

Very early one morning and still in darkness, somewhere in my unconscious I heard Uncle Tom's barge at our jetty and I thought that he would wake us all with the ship's whistle, of which he was so proud and which had terrorised most of the river dwellers for many years. However no sound at all came so I considered it to be a dream and dozed back off.

Mother was first up and I could tell all was well with the world because the smell of home-cured bacon soon permeated up the stairs and under my blankets, forcing my legs to leap out of the bed and straight into my trousers; eighteen-year-old boys get very hungry! Dad was in the scullery plunging his face into a large enamel bowl, filled with water just above freezing point and far below the temperature a young lad like me could endure without a large helping of eggs and bacon, so I was first to the table. 'I'm sure I heard your crazy brother first thing this morning,' said mum, but dad dismissed it by saying 'you'd 'ave known if it was that daft bugger, he'd have raised hell with that bloody whistle of his.'

After breakfast dad was first out to see if there were any eggs. The hens had almost stopped laying at this time of year but there were the odd one or two some days, and anyway, it was part of the routine that took him past the cider shed and indeed into the shed for a small tot; the sun did not have to be anywhere near any yardarm for the Gloucestershire cider drinker. Father returned much sooner than expected and instead of an egg or two he was holding aloft a large and heavy cardboard case and a very large and silly grin.

'It was that daft bugger you 'eard mother,' dad said, 'and he's left some goodies for us.' Pineapple rings - twenty-four cans of pineapple rings - it was like all our birthdays had come at once, and mum and I had certainly never had pineapple before, though dad said he had it somewhere during the war. Mum was in raptures over this tinned fruit and ushered it into the scullery to be thought over very carefully. This was only half the surprise, and the best for me was yet to come. 'Our Tom left a note stuck in the lid of the case, see what it says Ma,' dad said. 'Dear Lionel, I know you are not busy at this time, and I need your boy for a few weeks to helm a butty so I'll pick him up on my way back tomorrow, Tom.'

The thought of spending time with Uncle Tom was one that filled me with excitement beyond belief, for he was the most flamboyant character in our family and renowned on the Severn from Stourport to Avonmouth. I looked at my father who was fully aware of my excitement at the prospect of working with and being around Tom and his boats. 'Mind you don't get in any scrapes with that daft bugger and you be mindful of young Julie 'cos if you gets womanising with him it'll get back to 'er and you'll be in big trouble.' Mum had a wry smile on her face at the suggestion of Tom and I getting up to mischief, for she knew it was a certainty.

The work was not difficult for me because I had been around all types of boats all my life and I knew every inch of the river and the canal from Sharpness to Stourport. That day was spent chopping kindling for the house, mending a hoop net and baiting some eel traps, and in the evening I walked to Julie's to tell her about the adventure that lay ahead. I cannot say she was overjoyed at the prospect of me spending my time with Uncle Tom. Yes, even the young women in the Severn Valley knew of Tom's mischief.

That evening I spent packing some of my traps in an old seaman's bag that either dad had brought back from his travels or that Uncle Tom had left here some years ago. Mum had got together some clean socks, a spare pair of cords, some jumpers and an old army greatcoat. Dad's contribution was a sack with some skinned eels and two skinned-out rabbits. Night could not come soon enough for me because I knew that Tom would be on our jetty at about 9.00a.m. if he had got the first lock out at Gloucester. Dad said 'you'll hear that daft bugger coming two miles downriver because he will know you're waiting and he'll blow that silly, bloody whistle at everything.'

At 8.00a.m. I first heard his whistle. It must have been for the lady at Wainloads hanging out her washing. If it was the one I am thinking of, she, like many others, had had Tom's fingerprints on the cheeks of her bottom more than once! I collected my traps together, the seabag over my shoulder, and, with a goodly sum of beer money in my pocket, I was ready for the adventure.

Old Joshua and his wife were both dead now and Tom and Pansy had long since taken over the business which by this time was quite large and successful. They owned about ten craft in all, ranging from a barge called *Pansy* that sported a Lister engine, to three steam-powered narrow boats and six butty boats which were non-powered narrow boats for towing. Most families had now given up the practice of living on small narrow boats and

Haw Bridge.

had moved into housing, only sleeping on the boats if they could not get home that day.

Tom franchised some powered craft but also employed about ten bargees. The administration and the office work was undertaken by Tom's eldest son Ian and his mother Pansy because Tom refused to give up his life on his beloved river. This was especially so now that he had a new barge that was capable of carrying twice as much cargo as a narrow boat and able to tow two loaded butty boats, and what is more could be started with a starting handle and not a box of matches and did not need stoking with coal. Tom's barge was too wide for the small midland canals and was only used for the Gloucester and Sharpness canal and the river as far up as Stourport. The small company was well known and popular with shipping and transport firms, and always seemed to have more work than it could manage.

Pansy and Tom's children had all done well and one son was even at university in Oxford. One had a small shipyard in Gloucester and looked after many craft as well as his father's fleet. Two girls had married well and

View from Haw Bridge.

the beautiful Barbara worked in the office with her mother and brother. Barbara was as beautiful and wild as her mother had been; I am sure she would sooner have been a bargee than an office girl, and indeed she spent as much time as she could with her father on the boats.

Tom blew again at Haw Bridge just to make sure that they were all up at both the pubs. I could almost hear the friendly banter that they would shout back at him because Tom could get away with anything as he was the most lovable rascal known on the river. The first sighting was Jake standing on the bow of the *Pansy* with a head rope coiled in his hand ready to come alongside the jetty. The whistle started then and went on for a full five minutes while Tom waved a ladies corset out of the wheelhouse window.

Tom brought the heavy barge alongside the jetty and the head rope was made fast to a ring. Jake put a stern rope on and Tom walked up the gangway to the house. 'You noisy bugger,' dad said. Uncle Tom just smiled and headed towards mother who had flour in her hair where she had been trying to make it look its best to meet Tom. He lifted her up and gave her a big kiss on the lips before swinging her round and round until she screamed. Tom and Pansy were good to us now that they were quite well off and they always sent us nice bits of foodstuff and other treats, and took us out in their car sometimes. After some bread and cheese and a good old chinwag I stowed my gear on the barge and we set out for Diglis dock in Worcester.

Tom had been given a contract to move one thousand tons of tinned fruit from Sharpness to Worcester and Stourport, and eight hundred tons of animal feeding stuffs to Saul Junction. This was on top of his normal business which was keeping him very busy anyway. The problem was compounded by the fact that the mate of the *Pansy* was on the sick with a broken arm and ribs after falling into an open hatch at Avonmouth after a heavy bout of drinking with Tom some days earlier. But it is an ill wind that blows nobody any good because this was the reason that I was now mate of the barge and privy to the mischief she was always involved in.

Jake was the other member of the crew and a silent member he was too, because for some reason Jake could not or would not speak. As far as Tom knew he never had since he had found him wandering in Boardsley Green, Birmingham many years ago with no shoes on his feet and his clothes in tatters. The boy was about ten or twelve years old then, undernourished, covered in coal dust and showing signs of being beaten and neglected. Although the boy did not speak, Tom was sure by the way that he knew his way around a narrow boat that he was from a bargee-family and had been abandoned from some collier.

Tom took the boy in but despite his and Pansy's best efforts they could not find his family and no one on the waterways knew who he was. After a while the boy became very happy and contented and he was obviously very fond of Pansy and Tom, but he still could not utter a word. The first time the boy (who Tom named Jake) went on a trip to Birmingham, near the area where Tom had found him, he became very disturbed. The boy must have recognised the canal system on the outskirts of the town and he jumped from the narrow boat and began to run down the towpath in the direction from which they had just come. If someone Tom knew working on the bank had not stopped him, the boy would have run clear back to Worcester. Tom soon realised that the boy was too petrified to go into the Birmingham area and sent him back home with a family returning to Worcester docks. Jake was now about twenty years old but he could not read, write or speak, and would not leave the barge unless it was to see Pansy.

We berthed at Worcester at 6.00p.m. and walked the short distance to Tom's house and the warmth of Pansy's fire. Auntie Pansy was always so pleased to see me and always so welcoming. 'I have warned Tom that if he gets you up to mischief and into trouble I'll kill him, so don't you follow his daft antics,' she said. 'That's the only reason I've come auntie, to get into trouble,' I replied, and she gave me a big kiss and with a huge grin on her face she said 'you are too much like that bloody Tom you are!'

After a wash and a huge supper of neck of mutton stew we headed for Tom's local which was frequented mostly by bargees and other watermen; there were more miles covered in that bar than ever there were on the canals of Britain. The entry of Tom into the bar was like a breath of fresh air and most of the faces in the bar lit up on his arrival. 'God bless all here!' He shouted at the top of his voice. There were some very hard characters in the bar that were capable of biting the legs off donkeys as they ran past, but Tom could say anything because he commanded such respect from the rivermen and was greatly admired by all.

'What's all you bilge rats wasting your time in here for?' Tom said. We coughed our way through the pipe smoke to a small table in the corner where a little man who strongly resembled a last season's walnut sat smoking an old clay pipe and clutching a stone cider mug. 'How are you Wilf?' Tom asked. 'Too bloody far inland for my liking lad, nothing up yer but rain and cabbages. Do you know these bastards would drown the world for a bloody cabbage up yer, always wanting rain for the bloody gardens!' Wilf had been at sea for fifty years and could no longer get a berth so had been forced to live with his brother at Worcester. We sat for hours drinking cider and listening to the old man's yarns and seafaring tales before leaving to walk home. Halfway back Tom jumped over a small wall, banged on somebody's door, grabbed my shoulder and said 'run boy' and we were off down the lane like ten-year-old boys. Tom was in his early fifties and still could not stop his mischief, childish pranks and womanising – but that was what made Tom so attractive to everyone.

Next morning was a comparatively late start while the *Pansy* was being discharged on the quay under the supervision of Jake and one of Tom's maintenance men. We consumed a huge breakfast consisting mostly of bacon and black pudding from home that Tom would collect from our house. Three hours later and the sixty tons of canned goods had been unloaded and the barge bunkered and provisioned. 'I want to be at Saul Junction to pick up a butty and get to Sharpness by tonight,' said Tom. The butty is a dumb narrow boat or a narrow boat with no motive power. This is towed behind in narrow stretches of river or canal, and is lashed alongside in the wider parts and then it does not need a helmsman.

Early afternoon we passed my house without stopping but not without a prank. Tom had not used his compressed air whistle, which was usually responsible for the stampeding of cattle or bringing about the odd miscarriage, so as we slipped quietly past our house at full speed Tom unleashed a salvo of shots from his catapult. One shattered a pane of glass in dad's cold frame and one took the arse-panel clean out of his long johns that were on the washing line.

I pushed the throttle forward to escape the scene of crime as quickly as possible, but above the tortured sound of the over-revving engines I could still hear Tom's laughter. 'Ain't you ever going to grow up you crazy bastard!' Dad bellowed from the bank, whilst being aggravated further still by mum standing in the doorway wiping her hands on her apron and laughing fit to kill at the gaping hole in the old man's drawers.

Tom told me that the catapult with which he was an expert was a national treasure, and that when a well-placed pebble struck the bare arse of a fornicator on the riverbank, instances of unwanted pregnancy were greatly reduced in the counties of Gloucestershire and Worcestershire.

The bridge-keeper's wife at Saul Junction was the first that day to have her backside pinched, protesting wildly but loving it all the same, and wishing that Tom was staying longer instead of just picking up the butty and moving straight off again. After a small row with the bridge-keeper at Purton who said that we were too late for him to open - but because it was Tom he would let us through - we arrived on the old coal berth at Sharpness in time for supper. Ah, Sharpness! The maritime jewel in Gloucestershire's crown, a Mecca for seafarers, cider, loose women and the delights of the Pierview and Railway hotels.

Jake secured the vessels while Tom ladled out a stew that Pansy had sent with us and that Jake had warmed up on the stove coming down the canal. Supper over, we washed and changed into our best togs and left for the bright lights. Despite our best efforts Jake made it clear that he would not come, but Tom was used to this as he had tried for years to get him to go out without success. We walked over the high bridge to the Railway Hotel. Tom was a very attractive man with good teeth, a full head of hair and a stately manner about him. He always wore a leather waistcoat, cord trousers, a coloured shirt and a red neckerchief.

There were about seven ships in the dock, a collier from south Wales, a range of Dutch coasters and a large Polish ship with a deck cargo of timber, indicating there should be a good crowd in the pubs. As we entered the Railway a brassy old blonde woman with lipstick that made her look as if she was trying to swallow a postbox sideways rushed up to Tom and left a fair amount of postbox on his mouth. Tom diplomatically escaped the clutches of the old trollop and we moved to the bar. I ordered two pints of cider, wishing to keep up the tradition of a rotten liver by the age of forty.

We moved into a relatively quiet corner and joined some members of a Dutch crew that Tom had known for years and who had traded in and out of Sharpness and the Bristol Channel ports for a generation. Most Dutch crews consisted of a close-knit family who lived their entire lives at sea; the father was skipper, the eldest son was the mate and so on. The mother was cook and was assisted by her daughters or her sons' wives. These families were the cream of the seafaring world. They could somehow navigate by instinct and had an intimate knowledge of nearly every small port in Europe. They were truly master mariners and were respected as such; even above the Scandinavian and British coastal mariners. If you saw the tulip that they always had carved on top of the masthead you could be sure to get good advice on the entry of any port in Europe and its tides.

The Van-dar-Goot family had not been in their home port of Rotterdam for three years, trading between Hamburg, Dublin, Sharpness, and Le Havre, picking up varied cargoes from trusted customers and their agents. Their six-hundred-ton coaster, the *Wilhelmshaven,* had just undergone extensive repairs and refitting on the Clyde in Glasgow, and this was her first trip back to Sharpness. After leaving Glasgow she had sailed light ship to Dublin, loaded potatoes for Avonmouth and then light ship to Sharpness to load processed animal feeds for St Helier in the Channel Islands.

The skipper's name was Roll, and Tom had known him for years. They had met in other parts of the world while Tom was deep sea, and many times at Avonmouth and Sharpness since then. Roll was about sixty years old and loved cider, but always told Tom that it was not as good as Dutch lager beer to which Tom would reply 'your light beers are alright for girls and small children but I would drown before I got drunk on it,' which made Roll roar with laughter. To get his own back on Tom, Roll said – in his wonderful pidgin-English – 'is your willy still steering your course Tom?' as the tears of laughter ran down his weather-beaten old face, 'never had any of my daughters though did you?' He said. 'Ah! Didn't I ?' Tom replied, which made the old Dutchman laugh even louder.

The drinking and the banter continued until late, and during our stay it was noticeable that Tom had resisted any advances made to him from the gathering of what he called loose old tarts that frequented the hostelry. I think this had something to do with the fact that I was in his company. When the pub chucked out we walked with the Dutchmen back to the docks, and on the way Roll invited us for breakfast on the *Wilhelmshaven.* 'It won't be as good as Dutch bacon,' said Roll, 'but we will make do.' He could not help having a dig at Tom.

Next morning at 7.30a.m. we manoeuvred the butty and the *Pansy* onto the berth to load one hundred and twenty tons of animal feeds for discharge at Frampton-on-Severn. Breakfast on the *Wilhelmshaven* was wonderful and Monica, who was Roll's wife, was so kind and (despite her years) I think she was still attracted to Uncle Tom, kissing him as soon as we climbed the gangplank. We feasted on thickly cut Westphalia bacon that they had chandled in Germany some months before. I could see the flitch of bacon hanging in the galley, fried eggs and potato from good old England. The bacon was very good but not, I thought, as good as my mum's, though Roll said that next to Dutch bacon it was the best, and on that note I vowed to take some of mum's for him the next time we met. After some hearty handshaking and more kisses for Tom, we said farewell to these wonderful seafaring people to whom we seemed to have a close affinity due to their love of everything H2O - salty or fresh!

By 10.00a.m. the stevedores had loaded the two boats and Jake had rolled the tarpaulin over the hold of the butty and replaced the hatch covers on the barge. Tom checked the trim of the boats and we were off to Frampton. Tom was at the helm of the barge and I was at the tiller of the narrow boat on tow ten yards astern. It was quite an uneventful trip, a bit of catapulting, some rude gestures to other boatmen and plenty of saucy comments to bridge-men's wives and women on the towpath. This was the norm, until we got to the bridge at the Cambridge Arms where Tom spotted that the bridge-man's wife was opening the bridge. This meant that the bridge-man had gone out and left her in charge, and she was no stranger to Tom's affections, and, I think, even looked for them.

All within the time it took for the two craft to pass through the bridge, Tom had pushed Jake to the helm of the Pansy, ran up the deck, jumped off the bow, run along the open bridge, kissed and fondled the amply proportioned woman, run the remaining length of the open bridge and jumped on to the stern of the narrow boat as it left the far end of the bridge opening. This was all done while both boats were fully under way, and by a man in his early fifties. 'What happens on the boats stays on the boats mind boy,' he said to me with a huge grin on his face.

The generously built lady still had not closed the bridge when we rounded the next bend. All I could see was her cherry-red face, flushed with excitement more than embarrassment, as she adjusted her upper garments. Jake took all Tom's clowning, fornication and mischief for granted because he had had ten years of it, and anything Tom did was alright with him.

We made good time and berthed at Frampton mid afternoon, but the bad news was that they could only discharge the butty, and so the *Pansy* would have to wait till 7.00a.m following morning, which was a shame as we could have been back in Sharpness in time to see the Van-dar-Goot family before they locked out on the morning's tide.

A night stopover in Frampton meant a visit to the Bell Inn on Frampton green, run by a manic Irishman called Finnbar. He had been the all-Ireland bare-knuckle boxing champion and insisted on showing us that he could still do handstands against the bar wall at the age of eighty-two. How bizarre, I thought, but I was soon to discover that there was more to come.

Finnbar's father had managed to bring his wife and children to England to escape the ravages of the potato famine in Ireland, but not before he had set fire to the outside toilet of a wealthy and unsympathetic English landowner, not realizing he was inside. However, as there were no witnesses to the destruction of the privy, or to the embarrassment of the user, Finnbar's father escaped undetected, stowed his family on a friend's fishing boat and was landed at Fishguard with only the rags they stood in.

The family were taken in by a Welsh farming family and given food and a barn to sleep in. Later a cottage on the farm was provided and full-time work for Finnbar's father made the family better off than they had ever been in Ireland. The family stayed at the farm for the rest of their lives, but as a teenager Finnbar returned to Ireland and took up the noble art of bare-knuckle fighting for which he became famous. How on earth he ended up back in England as landlord of the Bell Inn at Frampton remains a mystery.

Finnbar's wife was famous for her hocks of bacon that she boiled up in a huge cauldron with cabbage, large unpeeled potatoes and some secret Irish herbs known only to her and four million other Colleens. They were the best you ever tasted. Tom and I had a helping of hock and she put some in a bowl for us to take back to Jake. 'How is the poor wee feller?' She asked. 'He's fine, I just wish I could get him to come ashore,' said Tom. 'Ah, you've done your best by him Tom and you're a good man yourself, but you're an awful wild bastard and I think you should have been born a Paddy man.' Tom knew most of the locals and we endured the gardeners saying it was too cold, and the salmon fishermen moaning that the salmon and elvers would be in short supply this year. Six pints of rough cider dulled the pain sufficiently for us to still have a laugh before we lurched and wobbled our way back to the boats.

The *Pansy* was discharged with the help of a rather rusty old auger, and by 10.00a.m. we made for Sharpness with all haste to load both boats with canned fruit before the finish of work that day to give us a clear run to Worcester the next morning. We were back in the port by 2.00p.m., just ready for the dockers return from lunch, full of bread, cheese and cider. It was a dangerous time to be working on deck but fortunately there was little for us to do and Tom only had to keep his eye on the trim to make sure they

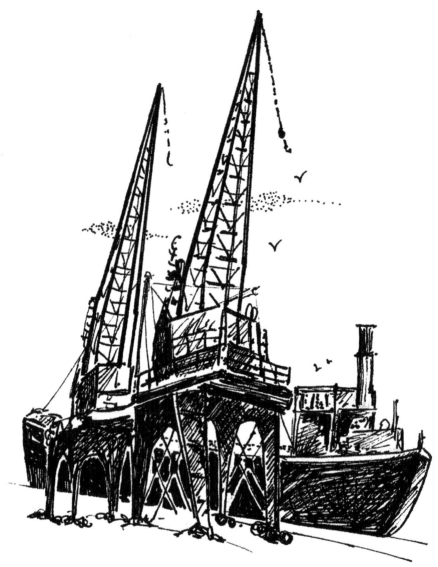

Puffer discharging at Sharpness docks.

did not load us down by the head. This meant too much weight forward which made steering difficult.

We were moored under the bow of a large Norwegian coaster unloading timber onto railway carriages. Tom went below in the *Pansy* and returned with a stone jar of dad's cider, forty English fags and two large tins of pineapple that he said was over-stow, and that it was not his fault if the checkers could not count. 'Stay here lad, I won't be long, I'm off to do a bit of trading with them Vikings.' Tom looked so much like a seafaring man that no one took any notice of him walking aboard any ship, and he went into the accommodation to find the mate or the boatswain to do his trading with.

Two hours and about three bottles of beer later Tom started down the gangplank with four bottles of Tuborg lager, some tinned crabmeat and, most prized of all, four large sides of toerag. Toerag is dried salted cod as hard as a board, with a smell that resembled the gents' urinal at the Pilot Inn at Quedgley, dead fish and an old lady who sold hats in Gloucester market. Tom hung three sides in the engine room and put some water in an old tin bath, dropping the remaining side in to soak until supper time. Tom was a great lover of toerag and he said that the Norwegians made the best in the world. 'We'll have a night aboard tonight lads, play some cards and have an early night ready for a sharp start in the morning.'

We busied ourselves about the boats for the rest of the day, cleaning, greasing and some red-leading on deck, always keeping a weather eye out for a drunken crane driver. Tom had been to the local shop and provisioned with some fresh bread, butter and some tinned peas. Washed, tidied and very hungry, Jake and I sat at the mess-room table waiting for the culinary delights Tom had promised us. The water soaking the toerag had been changed two or three times, and by now the fish had taken on a very different look. It was now pure white, twice the thickness, with a fluffy texture and no smell at all. The cod that this one side of toerag came from must have weighed at least fifteen pounds when it was alive, as this one fillet contained enough fish to feed a large family.

Tom warmed up two tins of processed peas and placed a large skillet on the galley stove. He melted salty butter on it, dried the cod off in an old engine cloth and coated it in more butter before tossing it onto the skillet. He fried the cod both sides for about three minutes before serving it to us with a generous helping of peas. Tom was right, this was the best fish I had ever tasted, and with the accompaniment of a bottle of Touborg lager we were left with a warm and satisfied glow.

The accommodation on the *Pansy* was in the forecastle, and with the heat of the galley stove it became very hot so Tom opened a porthole for some fresh air and we continued our card school. At about 11.00p.m. the result of dad's cider could be heard coming from the Viking ship in the form of some Norwegian sea shanties accompanied by a type of penny whistle. Every verse began with 'urdy, gurdy, burdy, gurdy, gurdy,' or that is how it sounded to me! Although they did sometimes throw in the mention of the god Odin and the name of some unpronounceable Norwegian fjord.

The Coalhouse Inn, Apperley, 2009.

We were on the move at 6.30a.m. and blowing for the first bridge at Purton to be opened at 7.00a.m. The *Pansy* and her butty boat made good time up the canal and we locked out into the river at Gloucester by lunchtime. There was a lot of fresh rainwater coming downstream, which made for hard going with both boats loaded to the waterline, but Tom was an expert and knew where to position the craft in the river to the maximum advantage. Tom began to blow the whistle one mile downstream from our jetty, frightening innocent bystanders and causing sheep to form panic-stricken swaths of white that moved at high speed over the green pastures alongside the river.

'I want your dad to be on the bank when we get to your place so that I can throw your mum a lump of toerag and a tin of crabmeat.' Tom said. With the noise Tom had made I expected to see the entire population of Gloucestershire in our garden. Dad was on the bank clutching another pair of long johns he had hastily removed from the clothes line on hearing the whistle. We could not moor on the jetty because we were too heavy and there was too much run in the water, which would have ripped the jetty from the bank. So Tom steered the boats as near as he could, gave the helm to Jake, and threw first a tin of crab followed swiftly by a large side of the salt fish which caught father across the shins, causing him to hurl further mouthfuls of obscenities at his brother.

Tintern Abbey and The Anchor Hotel in the early twenty-first century.

Tintern Abbey and the Anchor Hotel from a painting by Henry Harris in 1890.

Our small flotilla swung away from the bank as we made all haste for Worcester. I stayed as mate with Uncle Tom for another three eventful and exciting weeks, until the return of the injured crewman. I had had the best time of my life working and living with Tom, and I was sad when he dropped me off at our jetty on his way downriver, but in a way I was glad to be back home with a pocket full of wages and the thoughts of a cuddle with Julie…

CHAPTER THIRTEEN

TURKEYS AND CHRISTMAS TREES

Christmas was nearly on us again and dad had been asked if we would kill about a hundred turkeys for a poultry farmer just outside our village. Turkey killing usually started about ten days before Christmas so that they could be hung for a while, but the killing could go on until Christmas Eve depending on demand, so we were on-call to go any day.

With my pocket full of Uncle Tom's money I found myself at a crossroads in my young life. Julie and I had become very close now and were out and about together most of our spare time, and I was beginning to wonder what my life would be without her. I had many other interests in life and I had a number of good mates with whom I played cricket, skittles for the local pub team and got up to drunken mischief with, but it was with Julie I would prefer to spend my time. With Christmas coming and us both being just nineteen my dilemma was, would I buy her a ring and ask her if she would like to get engaged, or, being scared she may say no, go with my first thought which was to buy her a watch I had seen in the jewellers in Gloucester. I knew she would be over the moon with it because it would make her the only girl in our village with a wristwatch. My problem was solved on a pre-Christmas trip to Gloucester which we had organised some weeks before for the purpose of buying some presents for our families.

An old Leyland bus sighed with relief as it drew to a halt in the village and a conductress with a face like a smacked arse moved reluctantly to one side to allow us entry. We sat holding hands, Julie against the window and me in the aisle seat. The conductress, by now with a Woodbine clenched between her teeth, coughed her way up the bus, showering its passengers with fag ash and spit, and finally reached our seat. 'Yes, where to?' She snapped. 'Two returns to Gloucester please', I said, kicking myself for saying please but forced to by my upbringing. I paid the fare of 1s 2d and she threw two red cardboard tickets at me from a wooden contraption that hung around her neck and that I sincerely hoped would catch on a seat on her way back and throttle the old crone.

The old bus had been emitting a strong smell of burning rubber for some time. Then, just as we were crossing Westgate Bridge a jet of steam mixed with oil and water shot up through the wooden floorboards. A half-folded *Gloucester Citizen* the conductress was reading, the Woodbine she was smoking and two hundred multicoloured bus tickets were deposited onto the ceiling of the bus to form a soggy replica of the ceiling in the Sistine

Chapel. While the hag danced around the jet of steam, considering the bus's complaint to be terminal, Julie and I made a run for it. We sidled round the petrified hag, dodged the jet of steam and were off the bus in a flash laughing fit to bust.

As we walked briskly up Westgate Street, the problem I had been troubled by was resolved as Julie said, 'Farmer Hobbs, my boss, said that Moorhen cottage was empty and would get damp left unoccupied, and now that I was head cowman I was welcome and in fact entitled to it. What do you think of that then?' There was a strange inquisitive tone to her question, but I was sure I knew what she was trying to say. To evade the answer I know she really wanted to hear I replied 'good big garden there you know, old Ian Miller had it lovely at one time. Big the house is too, they brought up six kids in there.' Julie knew the cottage as well as I did, we had played with the kids that had lived there most of our lives. Realising I was being cruel I said 'would you like it then?' 'Not on my bloody own I wouldn't you fool', she said. 'Would you like me to come in with you then?' I asked. 'Course I would you daft bugger!' I gave her a long kiss outside the Shire Hall then, and I think that was my proposal of marriage.

We had a great day in town. Tea and lardy cakes in the bakers on Westgate Street, the cakes had so much lard and sugary syrup on them that they had to be prised out of the baking tray. I bought Mum a silk head scarf she had admired on previous trips to town but could not afford. She always wore one, and the one she had was covered in pulled threads from blackberry picking. We walked through the market and quickly passed the old lady with the hat stall who smelled like Uncle Tom's toerag and on to the fish stall that had a decidedly more pleasant odour.

Isiah Cornell was the fishmonger, but his name was not Isiah at all. I think his name was Basil but because he had a turn in his eye they said 'one eye's higher than the other,' hence the name! My father and his father before him had always dealt with the Cornells. They would buy all our elvers, eels, salmon and trout and gave us a good price. It was always a priority to stop and see them and they would always give us some herrings wrapped in newspaper and a few whelks for dad. Isiah's wife had a pie stall next to the fish stall and she would often serve in both, so sometimes your steak and kidney pie could have an air of haddock about it, but it was all good stuff. Their son George weighed about twenty stone and I think was no stranger to the odd pork pie from his mother's stall, but more than for his weight George was famous for singing to the customers whilst playing the spoons. They were a very happy and honourable family and a pleasure to visit. Loaded up with presents for our families and the herrings and whelks we made our way to the bus stop.

Mum was very pleased when we gave her the news of our forthcoming engagement. She liked Julie and her family and she had gone to school with Mrs Illes. Dad was an undemonstrative man but I know he was pleased when he said 'best young stockman round 'ere, 'er is, you'll do well with her, boy.' My next plan was for mum to contact Mrs Illes to see if she could get Julie's ring size so that I could go to town on the last Saturday before Christmas to buy the ring and hopefully get engaged on Christmas Eve in the Bell.

Next day the turkey killing started in the deep litter sheds at Brook Farm, a grisly business but one I was well used to and had been involved in from an early age. The twenty birds to be killed had been penned at one end of the shed by a farm hand and they were all large stag turkeys. The male birds are always referred to as stags and are larger than the hens, with a coarse wattle under their necks which was always left on after plucking. We had used this shed for many years and the hanging wire was left spanning the roof, with its hooks ready to receive the feet of the unfortunate fowl.

Father's trusty and razor-sharp knife would once again be brought into play. This wondrous medical instrument cut the skin off eels, the balls off pigs and sheep, the horn buds out of young cattle and was now about to relieve turkeys of their jugular vein. I am sure that some eminent surgeon somewhere would have been very desirous of this wonderful lancet. Big stags of around twenty pounds were difficult to catch and I would sometimes have to employ a form of rugby tackle around the legs to bring them down, which would ensure a liberal coating of turkey crap on the knees of the corduroys and the elbows of the milking smock.

When the bird was caught I would hold it at arm's length and high in the air by its feet, and father would slice through the jugular vein with the skill, and I might say the disregard, of Sweeney Todd. Then, in a move of great dexterity, I would pass the feet over to father and he would hang the bird on the overhead wire to bleed, which would keep the meat nice and white. This was a well-worked routine we had used for years and was efficient if somewhat gruesome, but life is hard in the country, and regardless of what the townies think, turkeys do not kill themselves or prepare themselves for the Christmas table. After the fowls had been left to hang for some time, some of the village women would draw, pluck and dress them for customers.

We had left Jenny nose-bagged and tethered in the yard. I took the nosebag off and filled a pail of water, she was thankful and seemed in a good mood. Part-payment for the turkey killing and other jobs carried out in the summer was to be a sack of the best King Edward spuds, a pail of milk, two large blocks of home-churned butter, a bag of rolled oats for Jenny and a good load of well-rotted horse manure for dad's cold frame. I led Jenny to the muck-heap and began to fork it onto the cart while dad collected the rest of the spoils.

Jenny showed her disapproval of having to haul muck by stamping her front hoof on the concrete yard and swishing her tail violently. Her disapproval was further endorsed by expelling the gases created by the oats in the nosebag just as I was collecting the reins from off her back to move her on.

We left the farm with the assurance that we would return to the killing shed when next required and made our way back through the village. We drew up at Nunk Deacon's house where his mother was scrubbing the front step. 'Hello Mrs Deacon, how's Nunk?' We asked. 'He's up the big house today doing a bit of weeding for the head gardener, he's good to the boy and gives us a nice lot of veg for the work,' she answered. 'That's great,' said dad, jumping down from the cart, 'I got a bit of butter for you 'ere and a nice few King Edwards.' 'Get on with you Lionel,' she said 'your family needs they vitals.' 'We got plenty, now you take this and say no more about it,' he said. 'Thank you very much, you're a good man Lionel.' 'Get on with you woman and I'll be seeing you.' Bill Deacon was a master carpenter and had been blown to pieces at Passchendaele .The poor woman did not even have a grave to visit and was left almost destitute due to that Great War.

We made our way back home with the smell of the freshly disturbed horse manure coming from behind and Jenny's wind problems from the front, both of which were vying for supremacy in the bad smell league. We forked the muck into a tidy heap beside the cold frames and went indoors for a much-deserved cup of tea and a slice of mum's caraway cake straight from the oven. While we sat father said 'I think we'll go to see Bert Illes tomorrow to get the cider and you can ask him properly about you and that cowgirl of his. I think you should come too mother.' I think mum was pleased about it because she knew that Julie was a good hard-working girl from a good family and would look after me properly for the rest of my life.

Next morning the traditional things were loaded on the cart; some rabbits, sides of salmon, bean sticks and some of mum's home-cured bacon. There seemed to be more than other years, a dowry perhaps! Anyway it seemed a lot for two firkins of rough cider. When I hitched Jenny to the railings outside their house, as I had done many times before, a feeling of fear and apprehension began to come over me and my bum began to resemble a very small pea. Everyone knew what was about to happen but it was still quite disconcerting as things like this were not much-discussed.

On entering the house shortly behind mum and dad, instead of my normal confident 'Hello Mr and Mrs Illes' I let out a tirade of undecipherable nervous twaddle. 'Our Julie is in the scullery, just come home from milking,' said Mrs Illes, my cue to disappear and seek the calming influence of Julie before I made a total arse of myself. I gave her a small kiss, squeezed her hand and 'once more into the breach' we went together. This seemed to me a ridiculous exercise as everyone in Gloucestershire knew of our intentions, but that is the way it was, I said to myself.

We stood close together, without any body parts touching, and I could feel my heart beating in my neck and my face reddening by the second. All four parents were stood to attention in anticipation of my proclamation. 'Mr Illes, Julie and me have, as you know, been walking out together now for some time, and we would like to get wed. Not right now but sometime next year.' By this time verbal diarrhoea had taken over and I was speaking so fast that each sentence was now a blur. Julie stepped in.

'My boss has said we can have Moorhen cottage, I got a good job and Alan's doing alright with his dad. There's no rent to pay for the cottage and it's in a good state inside and out. We got enough money for a bit of furniture and the boss's wife said we could have some bits of hers to get us started.' There was a lengthy pause and as the conversation had been, through tradition, mostly aimed at Mr Illes, he was first to answer.

'I'm pleased,' he said at length, 'you're a good hard-working lad, I know that from watching you with your father over the past years and I think you'll do well by Julie.' At this stage both mothers were wiping tears from their eyes on their aprons and smiling at each other with the most pathetic grins. All the parents seemed pleased but we knew that before this fiasco started.

The bartering for cider and net material, and the exchange of the goods we had brought with us was now done. Dad was nearly drunk like most years, but had held back a bit because mum was there, and we set out for home. While at the house I had asked Mrs Illes if she knew the ring size I needed to purchase, and she had given me an old ring that Julie had left off wearing to use as a pattern.

The turkey killing went on every day until the day before Christmas Eve, and our payment of the goods already received was enhanced by a sixteen-pound turkey with only one leg. The farmer told us that the bird's leg was lost in either a fight or to a fox, but I personally think that Splitter Cox had been around under cover of darkness one night and cut it off to use in some witchcraft ceremony. I suppose that the bird was unsaleable and the farmer saw this as a means to subsidise the cost of our work. We were well pleased with the spoils however, and it would make a change from the cockerel we had every year that dad would bring on for Christmas.

A week or so before Christmas one more job in our varied list of employments was always undertaken. It was one that was fun but unpaid. Every year since the war his Lordship had given a large spruce tree to be placed on the village green, and on Christmas Eve his lady and the vicar would lead the carol singing and she would give out bags of sweets to the

village kids. The tree had been felled by the woodsmen and was lying in the wood about two miles from the village. Father and I walked to Home Farm, passed the usual pleasantries with the farm manager and some of the lads, and went on about our business.

I tacked up a beautiful shire called Noble he was a good-tempered horse and always seemed to know what was required of him. We hitched him to a long hay cart that was brightly sign-written with Heskith Home Farm down the sides in red and gold over pale blue. We set off at a brisk walk and I instantly thought how strange it was to be sat behind a horse that walks without playing the Trumpet Voluntary through its bottom and without having to drive with the lapels of your coat tightly wrapped around your nose.

The tree was at least twenty feet tall and the woodsmen had felled it into a ride for easy collection. We backed the cart up to the thick end of the trunk and it took all our strength to lift the end onto the back of the cart. With our shoulders under the trunk we gradually eased the tree bit by bit on to the hay cart. With the cut end of the trunk at the front of the trailer there was still some of the tree hanging over the back, but it was only the soft top bit.

A hole with a metal sleeve inserted in it had been dug in the middle of the village green many years ago, and was covered with a flat stone slab to prevent drunks throwing themselves down it on Saturday nights. We pulled the cart onto the green and by reversing the loading procedure we eased the tree from the cart and left the cut end of the trunk hanging over the mouth of the hole. Dad had a block and tackle in the cart and the planting of the tree was soon done, with some leverage from the block which was attached to the gate pillar of the rectory at one end and halfway up the tree at the other.

Our labours were being scrutinised throughout by old Splitter Cox, looking at us from over the gate that Nunk and I had nailed shut in the past. Dad turned to the old crone and with a wry smile on his face he said 'it's nice out today Miss Cox, I think I'll leave it out!' The old hag knew what he meant and turned on the heels of her old black lace-up boots mumbling obscenities under her breath and disappeared through her front door. 'I reckon she's put a curse on you.' I said to Dad. We hammered some tapered wooden wedges down into the metal sleeve to hold the tree straight and steady and made our way back to Home Farm.

Christmas day fell on a Monday and the raffle for a hamper, and other yuletide gifts was on the Saturday before in the Bell Inn. There was always a good crowd in and the landlady put on some bits of food so there was a good party atmosphere. It was therefore our intention to use this as our engagement party, knowing that most of the village would be there.

Turkey killing now over, the eel traps taken out of the river and logs piled to the roof in the shed; we were all set for a good Christmas. For me one job remained, to buy the ring that Julie had admired so much in the jeweller's window on the day we had gone to Gloucester together. Armed with all the cash I could muster, which was a goodly sum, I stood shivering on the bus stop at 9.00a.m. hoping for another encounter with W.D. & H.O. Wills' best customer, the conductress from hell!

The bus arrived on time and I was greeted with a huge smile and a pidgin-English 'good morning, how are you?' by a huge black man looking very smart in his new uniform. I took my seat without speaking, I was stunned into silence, this was the first black man I had ever seen that was not in a school book or on the front of a jam pot. I could not take my eyes off the man to the point of being rude. After a while the conductor advanced towards me looking down at his ticket board that hung around his neck.

'Hello sir, where would you like to go?' he asked me. 'Gloucester return, please,' I replied. 'Certainly, sir.' I thought, shit, I've never been called sir before! 'Cold today sir,' he said. 'Yes, but it is nice and dry,' I replied. The conductor told me that his name was Wilf and he was on this run now for good and that he hoped to see me again. After he had gone I thought, what a nice man and what a contrast to the hag we had encountered on my last trip to town. Over the years Wilf became a village hero, helping the less nimble on and off the bus and even getting shopping for some old people and dropping it off for them in the village.

I made straight for the jewellers and stood to attention behind a glass counter full of rings and fine jewellery. I was approached by a tall, thin man with a pinched expression and a charcoal grey suit that had been pressed so many times it shone like some of the jewellery behind the glass counter. 'Can I help you young man?' he asked, and I thought about the 'sir' that the kind conductor had used to address me earlier. 'I know the engagement ring that I want, and I have a pattern for the size and I hope that you have it in stock.' I said. 'It won't matter if we haven't, I could get it altered for you in a few days,' he replied. 'I can't wait a few days, I'm getting engaged tonight,' I said. 'You've left it a bit late, if I may say so,' he replied sharply.

By this time the pinch-faced, sanctimonious old windbag was beginning to get on my nerves. I pointed out the ring that I required and gave him the copy for the size. He pulled from his drawer a metal spike, the like of which I had only seen on ships where they were called a fid, and used for splicing rope. It was tapered and marked in rings to denote the size of a person's finger. He slid Julie's dress ring, which he looked at with some disdain, over the measuring device, removed it and placed it inside the ring we had chosen for the engagement.

'You're very lucky young man, this size will fit perfectly,' he said, 'that'll be fourteen guineas please.' Hell, I thought, this is the largest expenditure I have ever made in my entire life and represents most of my year's savings. My hand slid easily into my trouser pocket, but being taught always to be frugal I had great difficulty in extracting it with the required monies and handing it over to a man who appeared to me to be a replica of Uriah Heep. I left the jewellery shop heading for the bus stop and on the Cross I nearly ran into Mr Williams, the estate manager up at the big house. 'Going home boy?' he asked. 'Yes, I'm just going to the bus stop,' I replied. 'If you hang on five minutes I'll give you a lift back to the village in my car.'

I waited outside the tobacconist while Mr Williams purchased his Christmas supply of pipe tobacco and we walked together to his car parked in Southgate Street. We talked mostly about the work that dad and I did for him and country practices in general. He dropped me off just outside the big house and to my surprise he said, 'I'll be at the carol singing and at the Bell this evening. I'm very glad to hear you are marrying the Illes girl, she is the best stockman around here by far, and I would like to get her to come and work for us, but now you are going to live in Moorhen cottage I will never be able to get her away from her present employer!' 'See you later and thank you very much for the lift Mr Williams.' I said.

Mum thought the ring was lovely and started the old eye-wiping-on-the-apron trick, which made me enquire of her why she felt it necessary to cry every time she felt happy about something. I was sharply put in my place by being told it was a woman thing and I would not understand.

Mid afternoon Uncle Tom and Aunty Pansy arrived, accompanied by the beautiful Barbara and two of the other children, all dressed up and looking very smart. Tom had driven down from Worcester in his almost-new Wolsely car, and deprived of his ship's whistle he had honked the car horn all through the village. 'Daft bugger' Pansy had said to him, but she knew it would make no difference to his behaviour, and that he would probably honk all the way home too. Aunty Pansy gave me a kiss and said that she was very pleased about the engagement and that she had some good pieces of furniture we could have to get us started.

Tom and dad started drinking cider in our shed at about 5.00p.m. Although dad thought that Tom was totally mad and defiantly irresponsible they got on great together, and the laughter that came from the shed as they swapped yarns was, to say the least, positively raucous. Mum and Pansy talked of womanly things, mostly about the exploits of the children and the price of goods in the shops. There was also a good bit of gossip along the lines of 'did you hear about her from Tirley? Dirty bitch!'

At 7.00p.m. the scene was set. Most of the villagers congregated around the Christmas tree and the singing was about to start. It was bitterly cold but dry, with the sky showing every star it could muster. The lady of the big house had on the most beautiful fur coat I had ever seen and his Lordship was wearing plus fours and a huge tweed overcoat. Dad touched his cap at the couple and his Lordship made a point of speaking to him. 'Hello, jolly nice to see you here,' he said. His Lordship had respect for father and was well aware of the work and services dad supplied to the estate.

A young Cornish girl shivered her way around the village green, handing out carol sheets to everyone. The poor little girl looked perished, although she was well and warmly dressed, as were all the girls in service at the big house.

The vicar and her Ladyship started off the singing and the Cornish maid, having given out the song sheets, now began giving out small bags of sweets to the toddlers and young children. As 'O come all ye faithful!' rang out, and the cold night air pinched the cheeks of the little ones, I could see the drippers on the noses of all the men over fifty, glinting in the strong moonlight, and I thought to myself how wonderful village life is on the banks of our bountiful Sabrina!

The carols over, the young and very old made their way to their homes, while the remainder of the vicar's freezing flock made their way to the warm and inviting bar of the Bell Inn. Pipe smoke, cider and hot pies created the nosegay, and a roaring fire in the enormous hearth the heat. The old ones with emphysema and chronic bronchitis soon stopped hacking, as the heat of the fire soothed their respiratory tracts and the cider numbed their throats. The snuff-takers wiped the brown snot from their top lips with red handkerchiefs the size of the foresail of a tea clipper, and the young and healthy ones had pillar-box red faces.

Uncle Tom was on his fourth pint of cider because, much to the annoyance of aunt Pansy, he had slipped away under cover of darkness, through the carol-singing throng, pinching the bottoms of women he knew would like it and disappeared into the pub before the three kings had got anywhere near that stable in Bethlehem! Julie's family had congregated in one corner of the bar with Tom and his family and my mum and dad. Tom was leaning over Mrs Illes telling her one of his lewd and risqué stories which had turned her face the colour of the snuff-takers' hankies, but she, like everyone else, took no offence and laughed as much and as loudly as was decent.

We all talked and laughed while we thawed out and the atmosphere in the pub was warm and inviting. Some of the carol-singing mood had now spilled over into the pub and the booming aristocratic voice of his Lordship could be heard reverberating around the walls. Momentarily he left her Ladyship exposed and vulnerable and in a flash Uncle Tom was by her side. 'O my God,' said Pansy 'that daft bugger will have us all sent to the tower and beheaded.' Tom was whispering in her ear and the colour began to rise in her cheeks. 'That's it we've had it now,' said Pansy. Seconds later her Ladyship let out a raucous laugh more befitting a fishwife than an aristocrat, patted Tom on the back and with a wry smile on his face he returned to our family group. 'You daft bastard, I thought you were going to tell her one of your rude stories or pinch her arse,' Pansy said nervously, adjusting her ample bosoms with her forearm, to which Tom replied 'I bet she would have liked that!'

There came a loud banging on the bar caused by his Lordship armed with a pewter mug. 'Not only are we here tonight for the carol singing, but

Ice in the River Severn at Apperley in 1963.

I have also been asked to announce the betrothal of one of our outstanding future rivermen to one of the best young stockpersons in this area. My wife and I are best pleased and congratulate the families most heartily.' I jumped to my feet and touched my forelock, as I had seen father do all my life, and said 'thank you very much sir,' and quickly sat back down on an old wooden settle as my legs had turned to jelly. 'Well done,' said father, nearly raising a smile. I was congratulated by Mr Williams, the farm manager, and his wife told me how lucky I was to be marrying such a beautiful and talented young woman.

Julie loved the ring that I had placed on her finger when we all arrived in the pub, but she had disturbed me by kissing me on the lips in front of everyone. I was sure we would be sent to hell for such a public display of affection, and all Uncle Tom could do was place the palm of his hand on his elbow joint and move his forearm up and down in a very rude gesture

Canoeists on the River Severn, still much used for leisure.

aimed at me from behind Pansy's back. The fun and drinking went on well past legal closing time, but as the local constable was drunker than most it did not seem to matter. This was the best night I had ever had, and the future for a nearly time-served river hobbler looked rosy.

The Romans had named my beautiful River Severn the Sabrina, while my forefathers were still wearing skins and blue paint. How wonderful she must have been for those men, so used to beautiful things, to give her such a pretty name. My year had turned full circle, and in a few weeks from now in this very pub some old man would say, 'I know they elvers is coming, I can smell 'um,' and a whole new year would begin on the river.

Appendix

Chronology of Seasons for the River Hobbler

Winter

Chapter 1 (Post-Christmas)
> Cutting logs
> Cleaning empty cider barrels
> Rabbiting
> Cider-making/delivery

Chapter 2
> Eel-catching
> Rabbiting (with ferrets and nets)

Chapter 3
> Skinning rabbits

Spring

Chapter 4 (March and April)
> Willow cutting (for basket-makers and salmon putchers)

Chapter 5 (April)
> Elver fishing and selling

Chapter 6
> Transporting cargo

Summer

Chapter 7 (May)
> Willow/perch cutting
> Salmon Fishing

Chapter 8 (May)
> Transporting a bull between two farms for bulling

Chapter 9 (May)
> Shad fishing

Chapter 10 (July/August)
> Pig castrating

Autumn

Chapter 11 (November)
> Apple hauling/cider pressing
> Cattle market
> Geese and duck shooting (wildfowling)

Chapter 12 (November)
> Working on the barges on the rivers/canals (transporting goods)

Winter

Chapter 13 (December)
> Turkey killing
> Planting the village Christmas tree

This chronology is a rough guide only. It should be noted that jobs can be carried out sooner or later in the year depending on the weather and the availability of alternative work.

Other flexible jobs included farmwork, gardening, cartering, and anything that could be undertaken for food or financial gain.

Other titles published by The History Press

Midlands Canals: A History of the Canal Carriers
ROBERT DAVIES

The men, women and children of all ages that lived and worked on the Inland Waterways experienced a Spartan existence. They would often commence work at 4 or 5 a.m., before shovelling out of the boat nearly 20 tons of coal, boating until well after dark. Many boats contained a whole family that would live, cook and sleep using a tiny cabin at the rear. This superbly researched and illustrated book spans the 1930s to 1960s, a time when transport of goods and materials went through great changes.

978 0 7524 3910 5

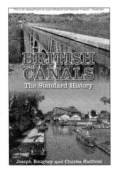

British Canals: The Standard History
JOSEPH BOUGHEY

The first edition of British Canals was published in 1950 and was much admired as a pioneering work in transport history. Joseph Boughey, with the advice of Charles Hadfield, has previously revised and updated the perennially popular material to reflect more recent changes. For this ninth edition, Joseph Boughey discusses the many new discoveries and advances in the world of canals around Britain, inevitably focussing on the twentieth century to a far greater extent than in any previous edition of this book.

978 07524 4667 7

Wilts and Berks Canal Revisited
DOUG SMALL

The Wilts & Berks Canal was opened in 1810 but promoted from 1793. Abandoned in 1914, urban development took its toll on the canal and in some of the country areas it was returned to agricultural use. But the rural nature of this navigation was in many ways its salvation, meaning much of it lay undisturbed. Since 1977 the canal has been under active restoration and is now the biggest project of its type in the country. With over 180 photographs and informative captions, Doug Small revisits this much-loved waterway.

978 07524 5146 6

The Bridgwater and Taunton Canal: By Waterway to Taunton
TONY HASKELL

A canal to connect the Bristol and English Channels was envisioned in Somerset at the height of England's 'canal mania' in order to save ships from having to navigate around the hazardous Cornish coast. Sadly this vision was never completed but the section linking Bridgwater and Taunton opened in 1827. By the First World War it lay it a state of decline until the mid-1990s when, following years of dedication and hard work, craft were once again seen on the restored Bridgwater and Taunton Waterway.

978 0 7524 4267 8

Visit our website and discover thousands of other History Press books.
www.thehistorypress.co.uk